A scene from Part One of The Royal Shakespeare Company's production of "The Life and Adventures of Nicholas Nickleby." Setting by John Napier and Dermot Hayes. Costumes by John Napier.

The Life and Adventures of NICHOLAS NICKLEBY

By Charles Dickens
Adapted for the stage by David Edgar

PART ONE

★

★

DRAMATISTS PLAY SERVICE INC.

SPECIAL NOTE ON MUSIC

The Royal Shakespeare Company production of THE LIFE AND ADVENTURES OF NICHOLAS NICKLEBY was presented by James M. Nederlander, The Shubert Organization, Elizabeth I. McCann and Nelle Nugent at the Plymouth Theatre, in New York City, on October 4, 1981. It was directed by Trevor Nunn and John Caird (assisted by Leon Rubin); the designers were John Napier and Dermot Hayes; costumes were by John Napier; and the lighting was by David Hersey. The American production was designed in association with Neil Peter Jampolis (sets and costumes); Beverly Emmons (lighting); and Richard Fitzgerald (sound). The music and lyrics were by Stephen Oliver; and the musical director was Donald Johnston.

"The Life and Adventures of Nicholas Nickleby"
is set in England in the first half of the Nineteenth Century.

Cast

(*in order of appearance*)

THE NICKLEBY FAMILY
NICHOLAS NICKLEBY .... Roger Rees
KATE NICKLEBY .... Emily Richard
RALPH NICKLEBY .... John Woodvine
MRS. NICKLEBY .... Priscilla Morgan

LONDON
NEWMAN NOGGS .... Edward Petherbridge
HANNAH .... Hilary Townley
MISS LA CREEVY .... Rose Hill
SIR MATTHEW PUPKER .... David Lloyd Meredith
MR. BONNEY .... Andrew Hawkins
IRATE GENTLEMAN .... Patrick Godfrey

FLUNKEY .... Timothy Kightley
MR. SNAWLEY .... William Maxwell
SNAWLEY MAJOR .... Janet Dale
SNAWLEY MINOR .... Hilary Townley
BELLING .... Stephen Rashbrook
WILLIAM .... John McEnery
WAITRESSES .... Sharon Bower, Sally Nesbitt
COACHMAN .... Clyde Pollitt
MR. MANTALINI .... John McEnery
MADAME MANTALINI .... Thelma Whiteley
FLUNKEY .... Richard Simpson
MISS KNAG .... Janet Dale
RICH LADIES .... Sharon Bower, Shirley King
MILLINERS .... Suzanne Bertish, Sharon Bower,
Lucy Gutteridge, Cathryn Harrison,
Ian East, William Maxwell, Sally Nesbitt,
Stephen Rashbrook, Hilary Townley

YORKSHIRE
MR. SQUEERS .... Alun Armstrong
MRS. SQUEERS .... Lila Kaye
SMIKE .... David Threlfall
PHIB .... Sally Nesbitt
FANNY SQUEERS .... Suzanne Bertish
YOUNG WACKFORD SQUEERS .... Ian McNeice
JOHN BROWDIE .... Bob Peck
TILDA PRICE .... Cathryn Harrison
Boys
TOMKINS .... William Maxwell
COATES .... Andrew Hawkins
GRAYMARSH .... Alan Gill
JENNINGS .... Patrick Godfrey
MOBBS .... Christopher Ravenscroft
BOLDER .... Mark Tandy
PITCHER .... Sharon Bower
JACKSON .... Nicholas Gecks
COBBEY .... John McEnery
PETERS .... Teddy Kempner

4

```
SPROUTER  . . . . . . . . . . . . . . . . . . . . . . . . . .  Lucy Gutteridge
ROBERTS  . . . . . . . . . . . . . . . . . . . . . . . . . . . . . .  Ian East
```

LONDON AGAIN
```
MR. KENWIGS  . . . . . . . . . . . . . . . . . . . . . .  Patrick Godfrey
MRS. KENWIGS  . . . . . . . . . . . . . . . . . . . . . .  Shirley King
MORLEENA KENWIGS  . . . . . . . . . . . . . . . . .  Hilary Townley
MR. LILLYVICK  . . . . . . . . . . . . . . . . . . . . .  Timothy Kightley
MISS PETOWKER  . . . . . . . . . . . . . . . . . . . .  Cathryn Harrison
MR. CROWL  . . . . . . . . . . . . . . . . . . . . . . . . . . . . .  Ian East
GEORGE  . . . . . . . . . . . . . . . . . . . . . . . . . . . . . .  Alan Gill
MR. CUTLER  . . . . . . . . . . . . . . . . . . . . . . . .  Jeffery Dench
MRS. CUTLER  . . . . . . . . . . . . . . . . . . . . . . . . .  Janet Dale
MRS. KENWIGS' SISTER  . . . . . . . . . . . . . . . .  Sharon Bower
LADY FROM DOWNSTAIRS  . . . . . . . . . . . . . . . .  Rose Hill
MISS GREEN  . . . . . . . . . . . . . . . . . . . . . . . .  Priscilla Morgan
BENJAMIN  . . . . . . . . . . . . . . . . . . . . . . . . .  Teddy Kempner
PUGSTYLES  . . . . . . . . . . . . . . . . . . . . . . . . .  Roderick Horn
OLD LORD  . . . . . . . . . . . . . . . . . . . . . . . . .  Richard Simpson
YOUNG FIANCEE  . . . . . . . . . . . . . . . . . . . . .  Lucy Gutteridge
LANDLORD  . . . . . . . . . . . . . . . . . . . . . . . . . .  Jeffery Dench
```

PORTSMOUTH
```
MR. VINCENT CRUMMLES  . . . . . . . .  Christopher Benjamin
MRS. CRUMMLES  . . . . . . . . . . . . . . . . . . . . . . . . .  Lila Kaye
THE INFANT PHENOMENON  . . . . . . . . . . .  Hilary Townley
MASTER PERCY CRUMMLES  . . . . . . . . . . . .  Teddy Kempner
MASTER CRUMMLES  . . . . . . . . . . . . . . . . . . . .  Mark Tandy
MRS. GRUDDEN  . . . . . . . . . . . . . . . . . . . . . . . .  Rose Hill
MISS SNEVELLICCI  . . . . . . . . . . . . . . . . . . . .  Suzanne Bertish
MR. FOLAIR  . . . . . . . . . . . . . . . . . . . . . . . . . .  Clyde Pollitt
MR. LENVILLE  . . . . . . . . . . . . . . . . .  Christopher Ravenscroft
MISS LEDROOK  . . . . . . . . . . . . . . . . . . . .  Lucy Gutteridge
MISS BRAVASSA  . . . . . . . . . . . . . . . . . . . . . .  Sharon Bower
MR. WAGSTAFF  . . . . . . . . . . . . . . . . . . . . .  Alun Armstrong
MR. BLIGHTEY  . . . . . . . . . . . . . . . . . . . . . . .  Jeffery Dench
MISS BELVAWNEY  . . . . . . . . . . . . . . . . . . . . .  Janet Dale
MISS GAZINGI  . . . . . . . . . . . . . . . . . . . . . . . .  Sally Nesbitt
```

MR. PAILEY .... William Maxwell
MR. HETHERINGTON .... Andrew Hawkins
MR. BANE .... Stephen Rashbrook
MR. FLUGGERS .... Richard Simpson
MRS. LENVILLE .... Shirley King
MR. CURDLE .... Hubert Rees
MRS. CURDLE .... Emily Richard
MR. SNEVELLICCI .... John McEnery
MRS. SNEVELLICCI .... Thelma Whiteley

SCALEY .... Ian McNeice
TIX .... Teddy Kempner
SIR MULBERRY HAWK .... Bob Peck
LORD FREDERICK VERISOPHT .... Nicholas Gecks
MR. PLUCK .... Teddy Kempner
MR. PYKE .... Mark Tandy
MR. SNOBB .... Christopher Ravenscroft
COLONEL CHOWSER .... Timothy Kightley
BROOKER .... Clyde Pollitt
MR. WITITTERLEY .... Roderick Horn
MRS. WITITTERLEY .... Janet Dale
ALPHONSE .... Stephen Rashbrook
OPERA SINGERS .... Sharon Bower, Andrew Hawkins,
                                        John Woodvine
CHARLES CHEERYBLE .... David Lloyd Meredith
NED CHEERYBLE .... Hubert Rees
TIM LINKINWATER .... Richard Simpson
THE MAN NEXT DOOR .... Patrick Godfrey
KEEPER .... Alan Gill
FRANK CHEERYBLE .... Christopher Ravenscroft
NURSE .... Thelma Whiteley
ARTHUR GRIDE .... Jeffery Dench
MADELINE BRAY .... Lucy Gutteridge
WALTER BRAY .... Christopher Benjamin
PEG SLIDERSKEW .... Suzanne Bertish
HAWK'S RIVAL .... Edward Petherbridge
CAPTAIN ADAMS .... Andrew Hawkins
WESTWOOD .... Alan Gill

6

CROUPIER .... Ian McNeice
CASINO PROPRIETOR .... Patrick Godfrey
SURGEON .... Timothy Kightley
UMPIRE .... Roderick Horn
POLICEMEN .... Andrew Hawkins, Mark Tandy
MRS. SNAWLEY .... Janet Dale
YOUNG WOMAN .... Hilary Townley

UNDERSTUDIES

Understudies never substitute for listed players unless a
specific announcement for the appearance is made
at the time of the performance.

Catherine Brandon, Wilfred Grove, Katherine Levy

MUSICIANS

Donald Johnston — *Musical Conductor/Piano*
Mel Rodnon — *Flute*
Seymour Press — *Clarinet*
Ethan Bauch — *Bassoon*
Lowell Hershey — *Trumpet*
Robert Zittola — *Trumpet*
Christine Snyder — *French Horn*
Daniel Repole — *Trombone*
Sandra Billingslea — *Violin*
Karen Ritscher — *Viola*
Doc Solomon — *Bass*
Bruce Yuchitel — *Banjo*
Jack Jennings — *Percussion*

Wedding Anthem sung by Choristers from
St. Paul's Cathedral. Master of the Choir Barry Rose.

PLEASE NOTE:

Part One is approximately 4 hours in length with one intermission of 15 minutes.
Part Two is approximately 4½ hours in length with two intermissions of 12 minutes.

The first performance of THE LIFE AND ADVENTURES OF NICHOLAS NICKLEBY was on June 6, 1980 at the Royal Shakespeare Company's Aldwych Theatre, in London.

AUTHOR'S INTRODUCTION

On November 19, 1979, a group of about 50 people sat down in a large circle in a rehearsal room in Stratford-upon-Avon, to discuss the possibility of turning Charles' Dickens' vast, panoramic novel *Nicholas Nickleby* into a theatrical entertainment. This group consisted of a large number of actors and actresses, two directors, an assistant director, four stage managers, and a writer. Over the following months, this line-up changed: some actors left, others joined, the team acquired two designers, an assistant designer, a composer and lyricist, a musical director, a band, a script assistant, a lighting director, lighting and sound technicians, dressers and stage-hands. During this period, the performers had experimented, improvised and completed 20 research projects into aspects of early Victorian life; the directors had overseen these exercises, had discussed, organised and undertaken rehearsals; the writer had written. By January 1980 it had become clear that early hopes of a one-evening project had to be jettisoned; if we were to tell the entire Dickens' story (as we were determined to do) then we would need two evenings: as Spring approached it became clear that these would be very long evenings indeed. And by our opening night, June 5, 1980, we had two vast plays: the first lasting four hours, the second four and a half.

The opening of the play, at the Royal Shakespeare Company's London theatre, was not the end of the story. After a short run in the summer of 1980, the production was brought back into the company's repertoire on two occasions; the show was adapted for television and recorded in the summer of 1981; the stage production transferred to New York in the fall of that year. Each revival and transfer saw cast changes, the production developed, and the script was rewritten and (I hope) improved.

This is not the place for a history of the way *Nickleby* came about (there is a good one, written by Leon Rubin, called *The*

Nicholas Nickleby Story). But it is important to give some impression of the process, for two reasons. The first is a matter of simple justice. Most scripts are developed and improved by the directors and performers who work on them, but *Nickleby* was perhaps unique as a collaborative venture. The original idea came from the directors, John Caird and Trevor Nunn; the style and texture of the adaptation was created by the performers; the set and the score helped to define not just how the show looked and sounded, but the basic method of storytelling as well. The script published here is thus a collective possession, in a very real sense: it was created over nearly two years by the best part of a hundred people.

The second point concerns the extent to which it has been possible to produce an acting edition in the conventional sense. While I have tried to make clear, in the notes that follow this introduction and in the text, how the show was and thus could be costumed, set and staged, many of these decisions resulted from the specific conditions in which we worked (and indeed from our personnel). It is open to future companies to make their own decisions, based on their own resources.

Two further things should be said by way of introduction. The first is that *Nicholas Nickleby,* Parts One and Two, tells the entire story of a huge Dickens novel. One can imagine all sorts of good reasons for doing one part but not the other, or even for doing versions of the play which contain some plots but not others. But I would nonetheless beg producers to consider attempting the whole, because one of the unique things about our adaptation was that, unlike every Dickens film and stage adaptation (and most of the television serialisations as well), we did it all, because we felt strongly that the only way to represent Dickens' achievement was to display it in its entirety.

Finally, I am aware that the notes and stage directions in this text may seem woefully inadequate to companies used to the excellent documentation provided in most acting editions. I hope they will understand that in order to present such detail in a show in which at least 39 performers play round about 123 speaking parts in 95 scenes would require a book of at least twice this size. Luckily, however, producers are able to pur-

10

chase, at most good bookshops, a companion volume which contains the most comprehensive acting, costuming, staging and setting instructions, and a lot else besides. It is called *The Life and Adventures of Nicholas Nickleby,* and it was written by the English novelist Charles Dickens in the early years of the 19th Century.

The Life and Adventures of

NICHOLAS NICKLEBY

Part One

ACT ONE

Scene One

*As the audience come in, the Company mingles with them,
welcoming them to the show. Eventually, the whole company assembles on stage. Each member of the company
takes at least one of the lines of opening narration:*

NARRATION.
There once lived in a sequestered part of the county of
Devonshire, one Mr. Godfrey Nickleby, who, rather late in
life, took it into his head to get married.

And in due course, when Mrs. Nickleby had presented her
husband with two sons, he found himself in a situation of
distinctly shortened means,

Which were only relieved when, one fine morning, there arrived a black-bordered letter, informing him that his uncle
was dead and left him the bulk of his property, amounting
in all to five thousand pounds.

13

And with a portion of this property, Mr. Godfrey Nickleby purchased a small farm near Dawlish,

And on his death some fifteen years later, he was able to leave to his eldest son three thousand pounds in cash, and to his youngest, one thousand and the farm.

The younger boy was of a timid and retiring disposition, keen only to attach himself to the quiet routine of country life.

The elder son, however, resolved to make much use of his father's inheritance.

For young Ralph Nickleby had commenced usury on a limited scale even at school, putting out at interest a small capital of slate pencil and marbles,

And had now in adulthood resolved to live his life by the simple motto that there was nothing in the world as good as money.

And while Ralph prospered in the mercantile way in London, the young brother lived still on the farm,

And took himself a wife,

Who gave birth to a boy and a girl,

And by the time they were both nearing the age of twenty, he found his expenses much increased and his capital still more depleted.

Speculate. His wife advised him.

Think of your brother, Mr. Nickleby, and speculate.

And Mr. Nickleby did speculate,

But a mania prevailed,

A bubble burst,

Four stockbrokers took villa residences at Florence,

Four hundred nobodies were ruined,

And one of them was

Mr. Nickleby.

And Mr. Nickleby took to his bed,

Apparently resolved to keep that, at all events.

Cheer up, sir!

Said the apothecary.

You mustn't let yourself be cast down, sir.

Said the nurse.

Such things happen every day,

Remarked the lawyer,

And it is very sinful to rebel against them,

Whispered the clergyman,

And what no man with a family ought to do,

Added the neighbours.

But Mr. Nickleby shook his head,

And he motioned them all out of the room

And shortly afterwards his reason went astray,

And he babbled of the goodness of his brother and the merry times they'd had at school,

And one day he turned upon his face,

Observing that he thought that he could fall asleep.

And so, with no-one in the world to help them but Ralph Nickleby,

(*Mrs. Nickleby, Kate and Nicholas are emerging from the crowd.*)

MRS. NICKLEBY. The widow,
KATE/NICHOLAS. And her children,
NARRATOR. Journeyed forth to—LONDON!

(*And immediately, the company becomes the population of London, jostling and bustling round, past and through the Nicklebys, until we can see them no more, and the next scene has emerged.*)

Scene Two

The London Tavern. A public meeting. On stage, some seated, some standing, are the organisers of the meeting: Sir Matthew Pupker, Mr. Bonney, a Flunkey, several gentlemen, and, sitting a little apart, Ralph Nickleby. In and around the audience are representatives of the lower classes: in particular, a large number of Muffin-boys, who distribute muffins to the audience from the trays they carry round their necks. There are also a few policemen to keep

16

public order, and, as we shall discover, an Irate Gentle-
man and a Furious Gentleman as well. The Flunkey bangs
his staff for silence.

FLUNKEY. My lords, ladies and gentlemen. Pray give silence
for Sir Matthew Pupker, Honourable Member of the Commons
of England in Parliament assembled. (*Applause. The odd cat-*
call. The Police finger their truncheons.)
SIR MATTHEW. Good morning. It falls to me today to announce
the opening of a public meeting to discuss the propriety or otherwise of petitioning Parliament in urgent condemnation of the
appalling, deplorable, and generally heinous state of the Hot
Muffin Baking and Delivery Industry. (*The Irate Gentleman*
shouts from the audience.)
IRATE GENTLEMAN. Crumpets. (*Polite applause.*)
SIR MATTHEW. Ladies and gentlemen, in troubled times like
these, when naked riot stalks the frightened streets at home,
and overseas the Russian bear is pawing at the very vitals of
the Empire, there could not be a greater nor a nobler task than
this we face today. (*Applause. To stop it, Sir Matthew raises*
his hand.) So, Mr. Bonney will now read the resolution. (*Bonney*
stands, coughs, and reads.)
BONNEY. The Resolution. That this meeting views with alarm
and apprehension, the present state of the Muffin trade.
IRATE GENTLEMAN. (*Shouts.*) And crumpet trade.
BONNEY. ...that it considers the present constitution of the
Muffin Boys—
IRATE GENTLEMAN. (*Shouts.*) And crumpet boys!
SOME. Order—shh—
BONNEY. (*After a slight pause.*) ...wholly undeserving of the
confidence of the public, and that it deems the whole Muffin
System—
IRATE GENTLEMAN. Crumpet! (*Bonney turns to Sir Matthew*
in frustration.)
SIR MATTHEW. Now, what—(*The Irate Gentleman has*
marched up on to the stage.)
IRATE GENTLEMAN. Sir, I must protest.
SIR MATTHEW. I beg your pardon?

17

IRATE GENTLEMAN. Sir, I must protest and I must insist. I must insist and I must demand.

SIR MATTHEW. Yes? What?

IRATE GENTLEMAN. And crumpets, sir. And *crumpets*. Not just muffins. Crumpets. (*Pause.*)

SIR MATTHEW. Is that an amendment?

IRATE GENTLEMAN. It's a demand. And an amendment, too.

SIR MATTHEW. I see. Well, then. All those in favour?

ALMOST EVERYONE. Aye! (*One Furious Man, however, shouts.*)

FURIOUS MAN. No, no, a thousand times, no! You'll rue the day. (*And he strides out.*)

SIR MATTHEW. The ayes appear to have it. Mr. Bonney.

BONNEY. And it deems the whole Muffin and Crumpet system prejudicial to the best interests of a great mercantile community. (*Applause.*) My lords, ladies, and gentlemen: I must state that I have visited the houses of the poor, and have found them destitute of the slightest vestige of a muffin, or a crumpet, which there appears to be much reason to believe some of these persons to not taste from year's end to year's end. (*Boos and expressions of shock and horror: "It's a scandal", "This must stop", "Fancy that".*) It is this melancholy state of affairs that the company proposes to correct. (*During the following a certain amount of protest develops among those sectors of the audience who are in fact muffin and crumpet sellers themselves, and have thus far been sympathetic to the emotional description of their sad and miserable lot.*) ...firstly, by prohibiting under dire penalties all private muffin and crumpet trading of every description; (*Applause—dies down, and we hear Muffineers.*)

1st MUFFINEER. Eh?

2nd MUFFINEER. What's he saying?

BONNEY. ...and secondly, by ourselves providing the public generally, with muffins and crumpets of first quality at reduced prices— (*Applause—dies down, we hear Muffineers.*)

1st MUFFINEER. He must be joking.

2nd MUFFINEER. It's our livelihood!

BONNEY. ...and it is with this object that a bill has been introduced into Parliament; (*The Muffineers are striding up towards the stage.*) ...it is this bill that we have met to support;

18

1st MUFFINEER. What about the muffin boys! (*Some Muffineers have reached the stage. Others are throwing their muffins on to the stage. Some disreputable members of the audience probably join in too.*)

MUFFINEERS. So what about the Muffin Boys
　　　　　　So what about the Muffin Boys
　　　　　　So what about the— (*The Muffineers are roundly truncheoned by the Police for this anarchic display, and are ejected, as Bonney:*)

BONNEY. ... and, finally, it is the supporters of this bill who will confer undying brightness and splendour upon England, under the name of the United Metropolitan Improved Hot Muffin and Crumpet Baking and Punctual Delivery Company! Capital five millions, in five hundred thousand shares of Ten—Pounds—Each! (*Wild applause. Bonney accepts hand-shakes from supporters and wipes his brow. Eventually, the applause dies.*)

SIR MATTHEW. Well, thank you, Mr. Bonney. (*Pause. Something should have happened. Sir Matthew looks to Ralph Nickleby, who has sat, impassively, throughout the proceedings.*) Mr. Nickleby?

RALPH. Seconded.

SIR MATTHEW. All those in favour?

EVERYONE. Aye!

SIR MATTHEW. Carried by an acclamation! Meeting closed. (*And suddenly, Sir Matthew, Mr. Bonney, the gentlemen, and everyone else disperse, and Ralph walks forward.*)

Scene Three

Ralph Nickleby is greeted by his clerk Newman Noggs, a sallow-faced man in rusty-brown clothes. Noggs carries a letter. We suppose we are in the street, outside the meeting.

RALPH. Noggs.

NOGGS. That's me.

RALPH. What is it?

NOGGS. It's a letter.

RALPH. Oh. The Ruddles mortgage, I suppose?

NOGGS. No. Wrong.

RALPH. What *has* come, then?

NOGGS. I have.

RALPH. (*Irritated.*) What else?

NOGG. (*Handing over the letter.*) This. Postmark Strand, black wax, black border, woman's hand, C.N. in the corner.

RALPH. Black wax. I know the hand, too. Newman, I shouldn't be surprised if my brother was dead. (*He opens the letter and reads.*)

NOGGS. I don't think you would.

RALPH. (*Reading.*) Why not, sir?

NOGGS. You never are surprised at anything, that's all.

RALPH. (*Folding the letter.*) It's as I thought. He's dead.

NOGGS. Children alive?

RALPH. Yes, well, that's the point. They're both alive.

NOGGS. Both?

RALPH. And a widow too, and all three of 'em in London, damn 'em. (*Slight pause. Ralph looks at Noggs, who is looking neutral. Enter Mr. Bonney.*)

NOGGS. (*Unconvincingly.*) Terrible. (*Slight pause.*)

RALPH. Go home. (*Bonney coughs. Ralph turns to Bonney. Noggs does not go.*) Ah, Bonney. Put me down for 500, would you?

BONNEY. They'll nearly double in a three-month, Mr. Nickleby.

RALPH. I'm sure of it.

BONNEY. And when they have... You'll know just what to do with 'em. (*Slight pause. Embarrassingly confidential.*) Back quietly out, at just the right time, eh?

RALPH. Indeed. (*He notices Noggs is still there.*) I told you to go home.

NOGGS. I'm going. (*Noggs snaps his knuckles and goes out.*)

BONNEY. What a very remarkable man that clerk of yours is.

RALPH. Kept his own hounds and horses, once. But squandered everything, borrowed at interest, took to drinking... I'd done a little business with him, as it happens, and he came to me

20

to borrow more, I needed to employ a clerk . . .

BONNEY. Yes, yes, just so.

RALPH. So, then—five hundred, Bonney. (*Bonney goes. Ralph waves the letter. To himself.*) What are they to me? I've never even seen 'em. Damn 'em! (*And he too turns to go.*)

Scene Four

Outside and inside a house in the Strand. Ralph walks round the stage, as narrators describe his journey:

NARRATORS.
And so Ralph Nickleby proceeded to the Strand . . .

And found the number of the house . . .

And stopped,

And gave a double-knock, (*Someone bangs a stick twice on on the floor.*)

And waited for an answer. (*A dirty-faced servant, Hannah, appears.*)

HANNAH. Yes?

RALPH. Mrs. Nickleby at home?

HANNAH. La Creevy.

RALPH. Beg you pardon?

HANNAH. Name, in't what you said. It's Miss La Creevy.

RALPH. (*Waving the letter.*) But— (*A female voice from off.*)

MISS LA CREEVY. Who is it, Hannah?

HANNAH. There's a man here, wanting something. (*Enter Miss La Creevy, a small lady of 50 in a yellow bonnet, carrying a paintbrush.*)

MISS LA CREEVY. Who? And wanting what? (*Hannah shrugs, nods at Ralph.*) Oh, sir—

RALPH. Madam, to whom—

MISS LA CREEVY. Oh, sir, I'm Miss La Creevy, sir, I am a painter of portraiture in miniature, sir, and if I may presume to speak such, you have a very strongly marked countenance for such a purpose, sir, should that be your—

RALPH. Is there a widow lodging here? A Mrs. Nickleby?

MISS LA CREEVY. Oh, you're for Mrs. Nickleby?

RALPH. That's right. I am Mr. Ralph Nickleby.

MISS LA CREEVY. Oh, Hannah, what a stupid thing you are. Why, sir, yes, they have their apartments just across the hall from mine, just there, sir, and I must say what an extremely affable lady she is, though of course very low in her spirits, and the children too, most pleasant—

RALPH. Over here, you say?

MISS LA CREEVY. That's right, sir, but may I remark, that if you should ever wish to have a miniature... (*Ralph turns back looks darkly at Miss La Creevy, who retains sufficient composure to produce a small card.*) Perhaps you will have the kindness to take a card of terms. (*Ralph takes the card. With a humourless smile.*)

RALPH. Of course.

MISS LA CREEVY. Now, Hannah, go on, and announce Mr. Nickleby to Mrs. Nickleby.

RALPH. I thank you. (*Miss La Creevy goes out, as Nicholas, Kate and Mrs. Nickleby come forward. Nicholas carries a chair, on which Mrs. Nickleby sits. Hannah leads Ralph to them. Hannah tries to make a proper announcement.*)

HANNAH. Uh, Mrs. Nickleby, here's ... Mr. Nickleby. (*Hannah withdraws.*)

RALPH. Ah, young Nicholas, I suppose. Good morning sir. And, Kate.

MRS. NICKLEBY. That is correct, sir. These are my— (*Unable to get out the word "children", Mrs. Nickleby bursts into tears.*)

RALPH. Well, ma'am, how are you? You must bear up against sorrow, ma'am, I always do. You didn't mention how he died.

MRS. NICKLEBY. The doctors could attribute it to no particular disease. We have no reason to fear that he died of a broken heart.

RALPH. Hm. What?

MRS. NICKLEBY. I beg your pardon?

RALPH. I don't understand. A broken leg or head, I know of them, but not a broken heart.

NICHOLAS. Some people, I believe, have none to break.

RALPH. What's that? How old is this boy, ma'am?

MRS. NICKLEBY. Nineteen.

RALPH. And what's he mean to do for bread?

NICHOLAS. To earn it, sir. And not look for anyone to keep my family, except myself.

RALPH. I see. Well, ma'am, the creditors have administered, you say, and you spent what little was left, coming all the way to London, to see me.

MRS. NICKLEBY. I hoped... It was my husband's wish, I should appeal to you—

RALPH. I don't know why it is. But whenever a man dies with no property, he always thinks he has the right to dispose of other people's. If my brother had been acquainted with the world, and then applied himself to make his way in it, then you would not now be in this—in your situation. I must say it, Miss Nickleby: my brother was a thoughtless, inconsiderate man, and no-one, I am sure, can feel that fact more keenly than you do.

MRS. NICKLEBY. Well, well. That may be true. I've often thought, if he had listened to me... Yes. It may well be true. (*Nicholas and Kate give an uncertain glance at each other. Ralph clocks this.*)

RALPH. So, what's your daughter fit for, ma'am?

MRS. NICKLEBY. Oh, Kate has been well-educated, sir.

KATE. I'm willing to try anything that will give me home and bread.

RALPH. (*Slightly affected by Kate.*) Well, well. (*To Nicholas, briskly.*) And you, sir? You're prepared to work?

NICHOLAS. Yes, certainly. (*Ralph takes a newspaper cutting from his pocket.*)

RALPH. Then read that. Caught my eye this morning. (*Nicholas takes the cutting and reads.*)

NICHOLAS. Education. The Master of the Academy, Dotheboys Hall, near Greta Bridge in Yorkshire, is in town, and attends at the Saracen's Head, Snow Hill. Able assistant wanted. Annual salary five pounds. A Master of Arts would be preferred.

RALPH. Well. There.

MRS. NICKLEBY. But he's not a Master of Arts.

RALPH. That I think can be got over.

KATE. And the salary is so small, uncle, and it is so far away—

MRS. NICKLEBY. Hush, Kate, your uncle must know best.

RALPH. And I'm convinced that he will have you, if I recommend it. (*Pause.*) Ma'am, if he can find another job, in London, now, which keeps him in shoe leather . . . He can have a thousand pounds. (*Pause.*)

KATE. We must be separated, then, so soon?

NICHOLAS. Sir, if I am appointed to this post, what will become of those I leave behind?

RALPH. If you're accepted, and you take it, they will be provided for. That will be my care. (*Pause.*)

NICHOLAS. Then, uncle, I am ready to do anything you wish.

RALPH. That's good. And, come, who knows, you work well, and you'll rise to be a partner. And then, if he dies, your fortune's made.

NICHOLAS. Oh, yes? (*To his family, to cheer them up, but becoming convinced himself.*) Oh, yes, to be sure. Oh, Kate, and who knows, perhaps there will be some young nobleman or other, at the school, who takes a fancy to me, and then I'll become his travelling tutor when he leaves . . . And when we get back from the continent, his father might procure me some handsome appointment, in his household, or his business. Yes? And, who knows, he might fall in love with Kate, and marry her . . . (*To Ralph.*) Don't you think so, uncle?

RALPH. (*Unconvincingly.*) Yes, yes, of course. (*Kate goes to Ralph.*)

KATE. Uncle. We're a simple family. We were born and bred in the country, we have never been apart, and we are unaquainted with the world.

RALPH. Well, then, my dear—

KATE. It will take time for us to understand it, to apply ourselves to make our way in it, and to bear that separation which necessity now forces on us. I am sure you understand. (*Pause.*)

24

RALPH. Oh, yes, indeed I do. (*Nicholas embraces his mother and sister.*) Now, sir... Shall we go? (*Nicholas follows Ralph out one way, as Mrs. Nickleby and Kate leave the other.*)

Scene Five

The coffee house of the Saracen's Head. A table, on which Wackford Squeers is sitting, reading a newspaper. Near him is a little trunk, on which a small boy, Belling is sitting. This scene is set up during the following narration:

NARRATOR. And so the uncle, and his nephew, took themselves with all convenient speed towards Snow Hill, and Mr. Wackford Squeers. (*The narration is carried on by William, a waiter at the Saracen's Head. Two maids enter, and stare at Mr. Squeers.*)

WILLIAM. And in Snow Hill, near to the jail and Smithfield, is the Saracen's Head, and outside the Saracen's Head are two stone heads of Saracen's, both fearsome and quite hideously ugly, and inside, on this January afternoon, stood Mr. Squeers, whose appearance was not much more prepossessing. (*Squeers lowers the newspaper. We see him as the two maids describe him to each other.*)

1st MAID. He's only got one eye.

WILLIAM. While the popular prejudice runs in favour of two.

2nd MAID. And, look, the side of his face is all wrinkled and puckered.

WILLIAM. Which gave him a highly sinister appearance, especially when he smiled.

1st MAID. And the eye he's got's a very funny colour.

WILLIAM. Which indeed it was, a kind of greenish grey, in shape resembling the fanlight of a street-door, through which Mr. Squeers was glaring at a tiny boy, who was sitting on a tiny trunk, in front of him. (*And indeed Squeers and Belling are looking at each other. Belling sneezes as William and the maids withdraw.*)

SQUEERS. Hallo, sir! What's that, sir? (*The maids withdraw.*)

BELLING. Nothing, please, sir.

SQUEERS. Nothing, sir?

BELLING. Please, sir, I sneezed, sir.

SQUEERS. (*Taking the boy by the ear.*) Sneezed? You Sneezed? Well, that's not nothing, is it?

BELLING. No, sir.

SQUEERS. Wait till Yorkshire, my young gentleman. And then I'll give you something to remember. (*Belling is crying. Reenter William.*)

WILLIAM. Mr. Squeers, there's a gentleman who's asking for you.

SQUEERS. Show him in, William, show him in. (*William goes out. Squeers looks at Belling, who is still sniffing. Belling cringes at this look, and is somewhat surprised when Squeers sits on the bench, and puts his arm round the tiny boy.*) Now, dear child, why are you weeping? All people have their trials, but what is yours? You are losing your friends, that is true, but you will have a father in me, my dear, and a mother in Mrs. Squeers. (*William admitting Snawley, a sleek, flat-nosed man in sombre garments, and two little Snawley boys.*) At the delightful village of Dotheboys, near Greta Bridge in Yorkshire, where youth are boarded, clothed, booked, furnished with pocket-money, provided with all necessaries, (*Snawley checks Squeers' speech against a newspaper advertisement he carries. It is the same.*) ... instructed in all languages, living and dead, mathematics, orthography, geometry, astronomy, trigonometry, the use of the globes, algebra, single stick (if required), writing, arithmetic, fortification, and every other branch of classical literature. Terms, 20 guineas per annum, no extras, no vacations, and diet unparalleled, why good day, sir, I had no idea ... (*And Squeers has turned to Snawley and extended his hand.*)

SNAWLEY. Mr. Squeers?

SQUEERS. The same, sir.

SNAWLEY. My name is Snawley. I'm in the oil and colour way.

SQUEERS. Well, how do you do, sir? (*To the little Snawleys.*) And how do *you* do, young sirs?

SNAWLEY. Mr. Squeers, I have been thinking of placing my

two boys at your school.

SQUEERS. Sir, I do not think you could do a better thing.

SNAWLEY. At—£20 per annum?

SQUEERS. Guineas.

SNAWLEY. Pounds for two, perhaps? They're not great eaters.

SQUEERS. Then we will not be great feeders, sir. I am sure that we can reach accommodation.

SNAWLEY. And this is another boy, sir?

SQUEERS. Yes, sir, this is Belling, and his luggage that he's sitting on. Each boy requires two suits of clothes, six shirts, six pairs of stockings, two nightcaps, two pocket hankerchiefs, two pairs of shoes, two hats and a razor.

SNAWLEY. Razor? Sir, whatever for?

SQUEERS. To Shave With. (*Pause. Snawley takes Squeers aisde. The little boys look at each other.*)

SNAWLEY. Sir, up to what age ... ?

SQUEERS. As long as payment's regularly made.

SNAWLEY. I see. (*Slight pause.*)

SQUEERS. Sir, let us understand each other. Are these boys legitimate?

SNAWLEY. They are.

SQUEERS. They are?

SNAWLEY. But I am not their father. (*Slight pause.*)

SQUEERS. Go on.

SNAWLEY. I'm the husband of their mother. (*Slight pause.*) And as it's so expensive, keeping boys... And as she has so little money of her own... (*Slight pause.*) And hearing of a school, a great distance off, where there are none of those ill-judged comings-home three times a year, that do unsettle the children so ... (*Pause.*)

SQUEERS. And payments regular, and then, no questions asked. (*Slight pause.*)

SNAWLEY. I should...I should want their morals particularly attended to. (*William brings in Ralph and Nicholas.*)

SQUEERS. Well, you've come to the right shop for morals, sir. I think we do, now, understand each other.

RALPH. Mr. Squeers.

SQUEERS. Yes? What is it?

RALPH. A matter of business, sir. My name is Ralph Nickleby. Perhaps you recollect me.

SQUEERS. Why, yes, sir ... Did you not pay me a small account for some years ... on behalf of parents of a boy named Dorker who ...

RALPH. That's right. Who died, unfortunately, in Yorkshire.

SQUEERS. Yes, sir, I remember well. (*Snawley looking at Squeers.*) And I remember too, how Mrs. Squeers nursed the boy ... Dry toast and warm tea when he wouldn't swallow, and a candle in his bedroom on the night he died, a dictionary to lay his head upon ...

RALPH. Yes, yes. So, shall we come to business? You have advertised for an able assistant, and here he is. (*Squeers looks at Nicholas.*) My nephew Nicholas, hot from school, with everything he learnt there fermenting in his head, and nothing fermenting in his pocket. (*Pause.*) His father lies dead, he is wholly ignorant of the world, he has no resources whatever, and he wants to make his fortune.

SQUEERS. Well ...

NICHOLAS. I fear, sir, that you object to my youth, and my not being a Master of Arts?

SQUEERS. Well, the absence of a college degree *is* an objection ...

RALPH. And if any caprice of temper should induce him to cast aside this golden opportunity, I shall consider myself absolved from extending any assistance to his mother and sister. Now the question is, whether, for some time to come, he won't exactly serve your purposes. (*Pause. Squeers a little gesture. He and Ralph withdraw a little.*)

SNAWLEY. (*To convince himself.*) A fine gentleman, sir. That Mr. Squeers, a gentleman of virtue and morality.

NICHOLAS. (*To convince himself.*) I'm sure of it. (*Ralph and Squeers back.*)

RALPH. Nicholas, you are employed.

NICHOLAS. (*Delighted.*) Oh, sir—

SQUEERS. The coach leaves eight o'clock tomorrow morning, Mr. Nickleby—and you must be here a quarter before.

NICHOLAS. I shall be. Surely.

RALPH. And, your fare is paid. (*Squeers takes Snawley aside, taking money from and inserting something in a ledger. Noggs enters.*)

NICHOLAS. Well, thank you, uncle. I will not forget this kindness.

RALPH. See you don't.

SQUEERS. Mr. Snawley... (*Squeers, Snawley, the little Snawleys and Belling withdraw as Ralph and Nicholas meet Noggs D.*)

RALPH. Noggs.

NOGGS. (*Hands Ralph a letter.*) Mortgage letter's come. And Mr. Bonney says—

RALPH. (*Taking the letter and opening it.*) Oh, yes. I know what Mr. Bonney says. A matter of investment. (*He opens the letter and reads. Noggs is looking fixedly at Nicholas. Nicholas doesn't quite know what to do. After a few moments, to break the silence.*)

NICHOLAS. Um, I'm—

NOGGS. Yes, I know. (*Ralph pocketing the letter.*)

RALPH. And we're late. You'd best go home and pack, sir. Early in the morning, you heard Mr. Squeers. (*Exit Ralph and Noggs.*)

Scene Six

The Nicklebys' rooms. Mrs. Nickleby and Kate, carrying a suitcase, books and clothes, enter to Nicholas as he speaks:

NICHOLAS. And there was so much to be done,

KATE. And so little time to do it in, (*The Nicklebys quickly packing Nicholas' suitcase.*)

MRS. NICKLEBY. So many kind words to be spoken,

KATE. And so much bitter pain to be suppressed,

NICHOLAS. That the preparations for the journey were mournful indeed.

KATE. (*Putting a book in the suitcase.*) A hundred things deemed

29

indispensible for his comfort, Nicholas left behind,

NICHOLAS. (*Taking the book out again.*) As they might prove convertible into money if required. (*As Kate puts the book back into the suitcase.*)

MRS. NICKLEBY. A hundred affectionate contests on such points as these took place;

NICHOLAS. And as they grew nearer and nearer to the close of their preparations,

KATE. Kate grew busier and busier, and wept more silently. (*During the following, Kate and Mrs. Nickleby leave Nicholas, alone with his suitcase.*)

NICHOLAS. And bed at last, and at six the next morning, Nicholas rose up, and wrote a few lines in pencil to say goodbye, and resolved that, come what may, he would bear whatever might be in store for him, for the sake of his mother and his sister, and giving his uncle no excuse to desert them in their need. (*And by now, the Saracen's Head has reappeared behind him.*)

Scene Seven

> *The Saracen's Head. Squeers sitting at the table with a plate of eggs and ham. The two Snawleys and Belling sitting with nothing. A maid stands next to William, carrying a tray, on which is a jug of water, and a plate of one piece of bread and butter. Squeers is holding up a mug of milk. Nicholas stands apart, watching.*

SQUEERS. This is two penn'orth of milk, is it, William?

WILLIAM. S'right, sir.

SQUEERS. What a rare article milk is in London, to be sure. Now fill it up with water, will you?

WILLIAM. To the top, sir?

SQUEERS. (*Starting to eat.*) That's correct.

WILLIAM. But, sir, you'll drown the milk.

SQUEERS. Well, serve it right for being so expensive. Now. Where's bread-and-butter?

WILLIAM. Here, sir. (*He puts the bread-and-butter on the table.*

30

The little boys quickly reach for it.)
SQUEERS. Wait! (*The boys freeze. Their hands go back. Wiliam goes away. Squeers divides the slice of bread into three, as Nicholas approaches.*) Good morning, Nickleby. Sit down. We're breakfasting.
NICHOLAS. Good morning, sir.
SQUEERS. Now, boys, when I say 'One', young Snawley takes a drink of milk and eats his bread. When I say 'two', the older Snawley, and then three is Belling. Clear?
BOYS. Oh, yes, sir.
SQUEERS. (*Eating.*) Right. Now, wait. Subdue your appetites, my dears, you've conquered human nature. One! (*Snawley Jnr. eats and drinks.*) Say 'thank you',
SNAWLEY JNR. (*Eating.*) 'Ank 'ou. (*Pause. Squeers eats.*)
SQUEERS. Two! (*Snawley Snr. eats and drinks.*) Well?
SNAWLEY SNR. Thank you, sir. (*Squeers finishes his food.*)
SQUEERS. And—(*He is interrupted by the blowing of a horn.*) Oh, dear Belling, there's the horn. You've missed your turn. Come, my dears, let's bustle. (*And at once there is tremendous bustle, and, during the following dialogue, one of two things occurs: if there is a mobile truck available. it is brought on, and the company build on it, out of skips, tables, chairs and luggage, a representation of an early Victorian stagecoach; or the sudden, noisy entrance of coachmen, passengers, porters, flower- and newspaper-sellers and passers-by gives the impression that the coach has arrived offstage and is nearly ready to go. Either way, everything suddenly becomes totally busy and confusing, as Squeers marshalls the little boys, and Nicholas is collared by Noggs, who appears out of the crowd.*)
NOGGS. Psst.
NICHOLAS. I'm sorry? Mr. Noggs!
NOGGS. (*Handing him a letter.*) Hush. Take it. Read it. No-one knows. That's all. (*He is going. Mrs. Nickleby and Kate appear.*)
NICHOLAS. Stop!
NOGGS. No. (*Exit Noggs.*)
NICHOLAS. But—
MRS. NICKLEBY. Nicholas!
NICHOLAS. Oh, mother, Kate—you shouldn't.

31

KATE. How could we just let you go ... (*Squeers, dragging Belling, comes to Nicholas.*)

SQUEERS. Now Nickleby, I think you'd better ride behind. I'm feared of Belling falling off, and there goes 20 pounds a year.

NICHOLAS. Right, I, uh—

SQUEERS. (*Dragging Belling away.*) And, dear Belling, if you don't stop chattering your teeth and shaking, I'll warm you with a severe thrashing in about half a minute's time. Come Nickleby!

KATE. Oh, Nicholas, who is that man? What kind of place can it be that you're going to?

NICHOLAS. Well, I suppose—that Yorkshire folk are rather rough and uncultivated—

SQUEERS. (*Calling.*) Nickleby, God damn you! (*If the coach is onstage, it is complete, and its passengers are clambering on to it, with the Coachman sitting up front with his whip, the horn-blower beside him; or it is clear from waving passers-by and exiting passengers that its departure is imminent.*)

NICHOLAS. Goodbye, mother. To our meeting, one day soon. And goodbye, Kate.

KATE. You'll write?

NICHOLAS. Of course I will.

COACHMAN. Stage leaving! Stage leaving! Everyone for the stage, up and sit fast! (*And Nicholas climbs up on to the back of the coach, next to Belling; or he runs out past the waving passers-by. Narrators speak to the audience.*)

NARRATORS.

And a minute's bustle,

And a banging of the coach doors,

A swaying of the vehicle,

A cry of all right,

A few notes from the horn—

(*The horn sounds. The coach departs, everyone on and off it waving. If we imagine the coach, then there is a further line of narration:*)

NARRATOR. And the coach was gone, and rattling over the stones of Smithfield. (*And one way or another, everyone except Kate is gone.*)

Scene Eight

Miss La Creevy's house: Miss La Creevy with her painting equipment in front of her on a little table: opposite a chair on a little platform. This is set up as Kate speaks to the audience:

KATE. And on the second morning after Nicholas' departure, Kate found herself sitting in a very faded chair, raised upon a very dusty throne, in Miss La Creevy's room, giving that lady a sitting for a portrait. (*Kate sits on the other chair, and poses. Miss La Creevy painting.*)

MISS LA CREEVY. Well, I think I have caught it now. And it will be the sweetest portrait I have ever done, certainly.

KATE. It will be your genius that makes it so, I'm sure.

MISS LA CREEVY. Well, my dear, you are right, in the main: though I don't allow that it's of such great importance in the present case. Ah! The difficulties of art, my dear, are very great.

KATE. I have no doubt.

MISS LA CREEVY. They are beyond anything you can form the faintest perception of. What with bringing out eyes and keeping down noses, and adding to heads, and taking away teeth altogether, you have no idea of the trouble one little miniature can be.

KATE. The remuneration can scarcely repay you.

MISS LA CREEVY. Well, it does not, and that's the truth. And then sitters are so dissatisfied and unreasonable, that nine times out of ten there's no pleasure in painting them. Sometimes they say, "Oh, how very serious you have made me look, Miss La Creevy", and at others, "La, Miss La Creevy, how very smirking!", when the very essence of a good portrait is that it must be either serious or smirking, or it's no portrait at all.

KATE. Indeed! And which, dear Miss La Creevy, which am

33

I? (*Miss La Creevy beckons Kate, who goes to look at the portrait.*) Oh!

MISS LA CREEVY. Dear, now what's the matter?

KATE. Oh, it's just, the shade. Is my face, really, that—

MISS LA CREEVY. Oh, that's my salmon pink, my dear. Originally, I hit upon it for an officer. But it went down so well, among my patrons, that I use it now for almost everything. It is considered, in the art world, quite a novelty.

KATE. (*Returning and sitting.*) I am convinced of it.

MISS LA CREEVY. (*Continuing to paint.*) And now, my dear, when do you expect to see your uncle again?

KATE. I scarcely know. I'd thought to, before now.

MISS LA CREEVY. Hm. I suppose he has money, hasn't he?

KATE. I'm told he's very rich.

MISS LA CREEVY. Hm. You may depend on it, or he wouldn't be so surly.

KATE. Yes, he is a little rough.

MISS LA CREEVY. A little rough! A porcupine's a featherbed to him.

KATE. It's only his manner, I believe. I should be sorry to think ill of him unless I knew he deserved it.

MISS LA CREEVY. Well, that is very right and proper. But mightn't he, without feeling it himself, make you and your mama some nice little allowance...What would a hundred a year, for instance, be to him?

KATE. I don't know what it would be to him. But it would be unacceptable to me.

MISS LA CREEVY. He is your uncle, dear...

KATE. (*Stands.*) From anyone. Not him, particularly. Anyone. *Pause.*) I'm sorry. I have moved.

MISS LA CREEVY. It doesn't matter, dear. (*Hannah is there. Someone knocks.*) Now, who can that be? Yes, come in. (*Hannah steps into the room.*)

HANNAH. Um...It's Mr.—um...

MISS LA CREEVY. It's who? (*Enter Ralph Nickleby.*)

RALPH. Your servant, ladies.

KATE. (*Standing.*) Uncle.

RALPH. Hm. Where's Mrs. Nickleby?

MISS LA CREEVY. Hannah. (*Exit Hannah.*)

RALPH. Is it my niece's portrait, ma'am?

MISS LA CREEVY. Well, yes it is, sir, and between you and me and the post, sir, it will be a very nice portrait too, though I say it myself as shouldn't.

RALPH. Well, don't trouble yourself to show it to me, ma'am, I have no eye for likenesses. Is it nearly finished?

MISS LA CREEVY. Why, yes. Two more sittings will—

RALPH. Have them done at once, ma'am, for she'll have no time to idle over fooleries. Have you let your lodgings, ma'am?

MISS LA CREEVY. I have not put a bill up yet, sir.

RALPH. Then do so, at once. For neither of them's going to need your rooms, or if they do, can't pay for 'em.

KATE. Uh—uncle, we are moving? Where?

RALPH. I'm not yet sure where either of you will be placed.

KATE. Oh, uncle, do you mean we're to be separated? (*Hannah admits Mrs. Nickleby.*)

MRS. NICKLEBY. Brother-in-law.

RALPH. Ma'am. I've found a situation for your daughter.

MRS. NICKLEBY. (*Sitting in Kate's chair.*) Well: This is good news. But I will say it is only what I would have thought of you. (*Ralph about to say something.*) "Depend on it", I said to Kate only yesterday at breakfast, "that after your uncle has provided in that most ready manner for Nicholas, he will not leave us until he has done at least the same for you!" (*Ralph about to say something.*) Those were my very words, as near as I can remember, Kate, my dear, why don't you thank your—

RALPH. Let me proceed, ma'am, pray.

MRS. NICKLEBY. Kate, my love, let your uncle proceed.

KATE. I am most anxious that he should, mama.

MRS. NICKLEBY. Well, if you are, you had better allow your uncle to say what he has to say, without interruption.

RALPH. I am very much obliged to you, ma'am. An absence of business habits in this family apparently leads to a great waste of words before business is arrived at at all.

MRS. NICKLEBY. (*With a sigh.*) I fear it is so, indeed. Your poor brother—

RALPH. My poor brother, ma'am, had no idea what business

35

was. (*Pause. Mrs. Nickleby says nothing.*) The situation that I have made interest to procure for your daughter, is with a milliner and dressmaker.

MRS. NICKLEBY. A milliner.

RALPH. Yes, and milliners in London, as I need not remind you, ma'am, are persons of great wealth and station.

MRS. NICKLEBY. Well, now, that's very true. That's very true, Kate, for I recollect when your poor papa and I came to town after we were married, that a young lady brought me home a chip cottage bonnet, with white and green trimming, and a green persian lining, in her own carriage, which drove up to the door at a full gallop—at least, I am not quite certain whether it was her own carriage or a hackney chariot, but I remember very well that the horse dropped down dead as he was turning round, and that---

RALPH. The lady's name is Madam Mantalini. She lives near Cavendish Square. If your daughter is disposed to try the situation, I'll take her there on Monday. Now, I must—

MRS. NICKLEBY. Kate, have you nothing that you wish to say? To tell your uncle?

KATE. Yes, I have. But I'd prefer to speak to him alone.

MRS. NICKLEBY. Now Kate, I'm sure—

KATE. I'll see you out then, uncle. (*She firmly gestures Ralph out of the room.*)

RALPH. Then—I'm your servant, ma'am. (*Kate and Ralph leave the room, and come downstage together. Mrs. Nickleby, Miss La Creevy and the furniture leave during this dialogue.*) So? What d'you want to say?

KATE. I must ask one question of you, uncle. Am I to live at home?

RALPH. At home? Where's that?

KATE. I must—we must, me and my mother, have some place we can call home. It may be very humble—

RALPH. "May be!" Must be. "May be" humble!

KATE. Well, then, must be. But, my question, uncle. You must answer it. (*Pause.*)

RALPH. I'd some idea ... providing for your mother, in a pleasant district of the country ...

36

KATE. Out of London?

RALPH. Yes, I'd thought so, but if you're quite determined that you want to stay with her ...

KATE. I am.

RALPH. Yes. I had thought you would be. (*Slight pause.*) Well, I have an empty house. It's in the East End. Till it's rented, you can live in it. I'll send my clerk on Saturday to take you there. So—is that satisfactory? (*Kate is cracking.*)

KATE. I'm very much, obliged to you, dear uncle. (*Pause.*) Very much—

RALPH. Please don't begin to cry.

KATE. It's very foolish, I know, uncle.

RALPH. Yes, it is. And most affected, too. (*To Kate.*) Let's have no more of it. (*Ralph goes out. Kate goes out another way.*)

Scene Nine

Outside and inside Dotheboys Hall. A bare stage. Snow falls. Wind blows. Squeers, Nicholas, Belling, and the two Snawleys walk D. with the luggage. They stop.

NICHOLAS. Dotheboys Hall.

SQUEERS. Oh, sir, you needn't call it a hall up here.

NICHOLAS. Why not?

SQUEERS. Cos the fact is, it ain't a hall. (*As Squeers leads the party round to the side of the stage, Nicholas speaks to the audience.*)

NICHOLAS. A host of unpleasant misgivings, which had been crowding upon Nicholas during the whole journey, thronged into his mind. And as he considered the dreary house and dark windows, and the wild country round covered with snow, he felt a depression of heart and spirit which he had never experienced before.

SQUEERS. No, we call it a hall up in London, because it sounds better, but they don't know it by that name here. (*He bangs an imaginary door. Someone makes the sound.*) A man may

37

call his house an island if he likes; there's no Act of Parliament against that, I believe?

NICHOLAS. No, I think not, sir.

SQUEERS. (*Banging.*) Well, then. Hey! Door! (*From the darkness, Smike appears. He is about 19, but bent over with lameness, and dressed in ragged garments which he has long since outgrown. He pulls open the huge door, and the wind howls as Squeers strides into the house.*) Smike. Where the devil have you been?

SMIKE. Please, sir, I fell asleep.

SQUEERS. You fell awhat?

SMIKE. Please, sir, I fell asleep over the fire.

SQUEERS. Fire? What fire? Where's there a fire? (*During the following, Squeers, Smike, Nicholas, and the boys with their luggage move round the stage—as if passing along corridors— as the Squeers' servant Phib brings on a big chair and then a table to centre stage. This is the Squeers' parlour, and Phib goes out again to bring on a tray of brandy, glasses and water, placing it on the table.*)

SMIKE. Please, sir, Missus said as I was sitting up, I might be by the fire for a warm...

SQUEERS. Your missus is a fool. You'd have been a deuced deal more wakeful in the cold. (*From off, we hear the voice of Mrs. Squeers.*)

MRS. SQUEERS. (*Off.*) Squeers!

SQUEERS. (*Calls.*) My love!

MRS. SQUEERS. Squeers! (*By now Squeers is in the parlour area, the boys are standing in the corridor with their luggage, and Nicholas is between them, as if in the doorway, not knowing quite what to do.*)

SQUEERS. (*To Smike.*) There's boys. The boys, to bed. (*Smike takes the boys out, leaving their luggage, as Mrs. Squeers enters.*)

MRS. SQUEERS. Oh, Squeers. How is my Squeery, dearie. (*The Squeerses embrace.*)

SQUEERS. Well, well, my love. How are the cows?

MRS. SQUEERS. All right, every one of 'em.

SQUEERS. And the pigs?

MRS. SQUEERS. As well as they were when you went.

38

SQUEERS. Well, that's a great blessing. (*These sweet nothings over, Squeers leaves Mrs. Squeers and takes letters and documents from his pocket. As an afterthought.*) The boys all as they were, I suppose? (*Mrs. Squeers, taking the letters from Squeers and placing them on the table, glancing at one or two.*)

MRS. SQUEERS. Oh yes, they're well enough. But young Sprouter's had a fever.

SQUEERS. (*Taking off his greatcoat.*) No! Damn the boy, he's always at something of that sort. (*Phib takes Squeers's huge coat, and stands there, holding it. Squeers goes to the table, sits, Mrs. Squeers pours him a brandy and tops it up with water. As:*)

MRS. SQUEERS. Never was such a boy, I do believe. Whatever he has is always catching, too. I say it's obstinacy, and nothing shall ever convince me that it isn't. I'd beat it out of him, and I told you that six months ago.

SQUEERS. So you did, my love. We'll try what can be done. (*Slight pause. Mrs. Squeers nods in the direction of Nicholas, who is still standing near the door, not knowing what to do.*) Ah, Nickleby. Come, sir, come in. (*Nicholas comes a little further into the room.*) This is our new young man, my dear.

MRS. SQUEERS. (*Suspiciously.*) Oh. Is it?

SQUEERS. He can shake down here tonight, can't he?

MRS. SQUEERS. (*Looking round.*) Well, if he's not particular...

NICHOLAS. (*Politely.*) Oh, no, indeed.

MRS. SQUEERS. That's lucky. (*She looks at Squeers and laughs. Squeers laughs back. They laugh at each other. Meanwhile, Smike reappears. Mrs. Squeers looks at Phib, and snaps her head towards the door. Phib goes out with the big coat. Slight pause. Then, with a wink to Squeers, as if to ask if Nicholas should be given a drink.*) Another brandy, Squeers?

SQUEERS. (*Nodding back.*) Certainly. A glassful. (*Mrs. Squeers pours a large brandy-and-water for Squeers, and a smaller one for Nicholas. She takes the drink to Nicholas. Squeers is looking through the letters. Nicholas takes the drink. Smike stands, staring fixedly at the letters on the table. Mrs. Squeers goes and picks up one of the boys' bags and takes it back to the table.*) Bolder's father's short.

MRS. SQUEERS. Tt tt.

MRS. SQUEERS. But Cobbey's sister's sent something. (*Mrs. Squeers starts going through the boys' luggage, picking out the bits and pieces she fancies.*)

MRS. SQUEERS. That's good.

SQUEERS. And Graymarsh's maternal aunt has written, with no money, but two pairs of stockings and a tract.

MRS. SQUEERS. Maternal aunt.

SQUEERS. My love?

MRS. SQUEERS. More likely, in my view, that she's Graymarsh's maternal mother. (*The Squeerses look at each other. Then Squeers notices that Smike is very close, craning to see the letters.*)

SQUEERS. Yes? What's to do, boy?

SMIKE. Is there—

SQUEERS. What?

SMIKE. Is there . . . there's nothing heard . . . ?

SQUEERS. No, not a word. And never will be.

MRS. SQUEERS. (*The very idea.*) Tt. (*Pause. Squeers decides to rub it in.*)

SQUEERS. And it is a pretty sort of thing, that you should have been left here all these years and no money paid after the first six—nor no notice taken, nor no clue to who you belong to? It's a pretty sort of thing, is it not, that I should have to feed a great fellow like you, and never hope to get one penny for it, isn't it? (*Squeers looking at Smike.*)

NICHOLAS. (*Out front.*) The boy put his hand to his head, as if he was making an effort to remember something, and then, looking vacantly at his questioner, gradually broke into a smile.

SQUEERS. That's right. Now, off with you, and send the girl. (*Smike limps out. Mrs. Squeers has finished sifting the boy's bag. She looks for something on the table.*)

MRS. SQUEERS. I tell you what, Squeers, I think that young chap's turning silly.

SQUEERS. (*Wiping his mouth.*) I hope not. For he's a handy fellow out of doors, and worth his meat and drink anyway. (*He stands.*) But come, I'm tired, and want to go to bed.

MRS. SQUEERS. Oh, drat the thing.

SQUEERS. What's wrong, my dear?

MRS. SQUEERS. The school spoon. I can't find it.

SQUEERS. Never mind, my love.

MRS. SQUEERS. What, never mind? It's brimstone, in the morning.

SQUEERS. Ah, I forgot. (*He helps the search.*) Yes, certainly, it is.

NICHOLAS. Uh...?

SQUEERS. We purify the boys' bloods now and then, Nickleby.

MRS. SQUEERS. (*Crossly.*) Purify fiddle-sticks. Don't think, young man, that we go to the expense of flour of brimstone and molasses just to purify them; because if you think we carry on the business in that way, you'll find yourself mistaken, and so I tell you plainly. (*Squeers is not sure this intelligence is quite discreet. Enter Phib, who tidies round the table, putting things back on the tray.*)

SQUEERS. My dear...should you...

MRS. SQUEERS. Nonsense. If the young man comes to be a teacher, let him understand at once that we don't want any foolery about the boys. They have the brimstone and treacle, partly because if they hadn't something or other in the way of medicine they'd always be ailing and giving a world of trouble, and partly because it spoils their appetites and comes cheaper than breakfast and dinner. So it does them good and us good at the same time, and that's fair enough, I'm sure. (*Squeers looking embarrassed. Mrs. Squeers shoots a glance at him.*) Now, where's the spoon? (*Phib has picked up the tray.*)

PHIB. Uh. Ma'am.

MRS. SQUEERS. What is it?

PHIB. S'round your neck. (*And indeed the spoon is round Mrs. Squeers neck. She cuffs Phib lightly for telling her.*)

MRS. SQUEERS. Why did you not say *before*.

PHIB. M'sorry, ma'am. (*Phib picks up the tray, leaving the brandy bottle, and goes out.*)

MRS. SQUEERS. (*Pleasantly.*) And so, dear Mr. Nickleby, good night. (*Mrs. Squeers goes out. Pause.*)

SQUEERS. A most invaluable woman, Nickleby.

NICHOLAS. Indeed, sir.

SQUEERS. I do not know her equal. That woman, Nickleby,

is always the same: always the same bustling, lively, active, saving creature that you see her now.

NICHOLAS. I'm sure of it.

SQUEERS. (*Warming further to his theme.*) It is my custom, when I am in London, to say that she is like a mother to those boys. But she is more, she's ten times more. She does things for those boys, Nickleby, that I don't believe half the mothers going would do for their own sons.

NICHOLAS. I'm certain of it, sir.

SQUEERS. And so, goodnight, then, Nickleby. (*He tries to make a solemn exit, undermined by spotting the brandy, which he returns to pick up.*)

NICHOLAS. Goodnight, sir. (*Squeers nods gravely and goes out. Nicholas stands a moment, then takes off his coat. He sits, on the floor. He notices Noggs' letter in his coat pocket. He opens it and begins to read. Noggs' himself appears, with a glass of brandy. He sits on the arm of Squeers' chair, and he speaks his letter as we see Nicholas read it.*)

NOGGS. My dear young man. I know the world. Your father did not, or he would not have done me a kindness when there was no hope of return. You do not, or you would not be bound on such a journey. If ever you want a shelter in London, they know where I live at the sign of the Crown, in Silver St., Golden Square. You can come at night. Once, nobody was ashamed— never mind that. It's all over. Excuse errors. I have forgotten all my old ways. My spelling may have gone with them.

NICHOLAS. (*Reads.*) Yours obediently, Newman Noggs.

NOGGS. P.S.: If you should go near Barnard Castle, there is a good ale at the King's Head. Say you know me, and I am sure they will not charge you for it. You may say Mr. Noggs there, for I was a gentleman then. I was indeed. (*Noggs shambles out. Nicholas crumples to the floor. He is crying. Blackout.*)

Scene Ten

Dotheboys Hall. The school bell rings, the lights come up. The parlour chair and table have gone. Squeers shouts to Nicholas, who wakes.

SQUEERS. Past seven, Nickleby! It's morning come, and well-iced already. Now, Nickleby, come, tumble up, will you?
(*Squeers, with his cane, strides round the stage. Nicholas jumps up and, pulling on his coat, follows. Mrs. Squeers enters, followed by Smike, who carries a bowl of brimstone and treacle. Squeers and Nicholas arrive at one side of the stage, Mrs. Squeers and Smike at the other. Then, through the darkness at the back of the stage, we see, approaching us, the boys of Dotheboys Hall. They are dressed in the ragged remains of what were once school uniforms. They move slowly, through lameness and sullenness and fear. Then they form themselves into a kind of line, and each boy goes to Mrs. Squeers to receive a spoonful of brimstone and treacle.*) There. This is our shop, Nickleby. (*Each boy gives his number, name, age and reason for being at the school before receiving his dose. Clearly, this is an accepted ritual.*)
TOMKINS. First boy. Tomkins. Nine. A cripple.
COATES. Second boy. Coates. Thirteen. A bastard.
GRAYMARSH. Third boy. Graymarsh. Twelve, Another bastard.
JENNINGS. Fourth boy. Jennings. Thirteen. Disfigured.
MOBBS. Fifth boy. (*Pause.*) Mobbs. Uh—'leven. (*Pause. He doesn't know what's wrong with him. Mrs. Squeers hits him on the side of the head.*)
MRS. SQUEERS. Simpleton!
MOBBS. Fifth. Mobbs. Eleven. Sim-pull-ton.
BOLDER. Sixth. Bolder. Fourteen, Orphan.
PITCHER. Seventh. Pitcher. Ten.
MRS. SQUEERS. Yes! (*Pause.*)
PITCHER. I'm very. Very. Slow.
MRS. SQUEERS. Move on. Move *on*.
JACKSON. Eighth. Johnny.
MRS. SQUEERS. Johnny?
JACKSON. Jackson. Thirteen. Illegitimate.
COBBEY. Ninth. Cobbey. Fifteen. Cripple.
PETERS. Tenth. Uh—Peters. Seven. Blind.
SPROUTER. Eleventh. Sprouter. Seven. My father killed my mother.
MRS. SQUEERS. Yes?
SPROUTER. Sent away.

ROBERTS. Twelfth. Roberts. Ten. There's something wrong—my brain. (*Squeers' young son, Wackford, well-dressed and stout, pushes forward the two Snawley boys and Belling.*)

SNAWLEY SNR. Robert Arthur Snawley.

MRS. SQUEERS. Number!

SNAWLEY SNR. I'm eleven.

MRS. SQUEERS. (*Twisting Snawley Snr's ear.*) Number, is thirteen.

SNAWLEY SNR. Thirteen.

SNAWLEY JNR. Uh—fourteen-th. Snawley, H. Uh—seven.

BELLING. Fifteen. Anthony Belling. Seven years of age. A classical and modern—moral, education. (*Mrs. Squeers wipes her hands on Smike. Squeers to Wackford.*)

SQUEERS. Thank you, young Wackford. Thank you, son. And what do you say? And what d'you say, to this? (*Pause.*)

BOYS. For what we have received, may the lord make us truly thankful.

SQUEERS. Amen.

BOYS. Amen.

SQUEERS. That's better. Now, boys, I've been to London, and have returned to my family and you, as strong and well as ever. (*Pause. Mrs. Squeers gestures to a boy.*)

COATES. (*Feebly.*) Hip hip.

BOYS. (*Equally feebly.*) Hooray.

COATES. Hip hip.

BOYS. Hooray.

COATES. Hip hip.

BOYS. Hooray. (*Squeers takes various letters from his pockets and wanders around among the boys as he speaks.*)

SQUEERS. I have seen the parents of some boys, and they're so glad to hear how their sons are doing, that there's no prospect at all of their going home, which of course is a very pleasant thing to reflect upon for all parties. (*He continues to perambulate.*) But I have had disappointments to contend with. Bolder's father, for an instance, was two pound ten short. Where is Bolder? (*The boys around Bolder kick him and he puts up his hand. Squeers goes to Bolder.*) Ah, Bolder. Bolder, if you father thinks that because—(*Squeers suddenly notices warts on Bolder's hand.*

44

He grabs the boy's arm.) What do you call this, sir?
BOLDER. Warts, sir.
SQUEERS. What, sir?
BOLDER. Warts, sir.
SQUEERS. Warts?
BOLDER. I can't help it, sir. They will come ... It's working in the garden does it sir, at least I don't know what it is, sir, but it's not my fault ...
SQUEERS. Bolder. You are an incorrigible young scoundrel, and as the last thrashing did you no good, we must see what another will do towards beating it out of you. (*Bolder looks terrified.*) La—ter. (*He lets Bolder go and walks on, reading.*) Now, let's see ... A letter for Cobbey. Cobbey? (*Cobbey puts his hand up. Squeers hardly acknowledges, but walks on.*) Oh. Cobbey's grandmother is dead, and his uncle John has took to drinking, which is all the news his sister sends, except eighteenpence, which will just pay for that broken square of glass. Mobbs! (*Mobbs, not sure whether this will be good or bad news, nervously puts up his hand. It is clear it is not good news when Squeers walks to him and stands near.*) Now, Mobbs' step-mother took to her bed on hearing that he would not eat fat, and has been very ill ever since. She wishes to know by an early post where he expects to go to, if he quarrels with his vittles; and with what feelings he could turn up his nose at the cow's liver broth, after his good master had asked a blessing on it. She is disconsolate to find he is discontented, which is sinful and horrid, and hopes Mr. Squeers will flog him into a happier state of mind. (*Into Mobb's ear.*) Which—he—will. (*Long pause to let this sink in to everyone. Then.*) Right, boys. I'd like you all to meet my new assistant, Mr. Nickleby. Good morning, Mr. Nickleby.
BOYS. Good morning, Mr. Nickleby.
NICHOLAS. Good, morning.
SQUEERS. Now, this is the first class in English spelling and philosophy, Nickleby. We'll soon get up a Latin one and hand that over to you. (*Nicholas joins Squeers.*) Now, then, where's Smallpiece?
BOYS. Please, sir ...

45

SQUEERS. Let any boy speak out of turn and I'll have the skin off his back! (*He points to Jennings.*)

JENNINGS. Please, sir, he's cleaning the back parlour window.

SQUEERS. So he is, to be sure. We go on the practical mode of teaching, Nickleby; C-l-e-a-n, clean—

BOYS. Clean.

SQUEERS. verb active, to make bright, to scour. W-i-n, win,—

BOYS. Win—

SQUEERS. d-e-r, der—

BOYS. der, winder—

SQUEERS. Winder, a casement. When a boy knows this out of a book, he goes and does it. It's just the same principle as the use of the globes. Where's Grinder? (*Coates puts his hand up. Squeers points to Coates.*)

COATES. Please, sir, he's weeding the garden.

SQUEERS. To be sure. So he is. B-o-t, Bot—

BOYS. Bot—

SQUEERS. T-i-n, tin—

BOYS. Tin—

SQUEERS. Bottin—

BOYS. Bottin—

SQUEERS. N-e-y, Ney—

BOYS. Ney—

SQUEERS. Bottiney—

BOYS. Bottiney—

SQUEERS. Noun substantive, a knowledge of plants. When he has learned that bottiney means a knowledge of plants, he goes and knows 'em. That's our system, Nickleby. What do you think of it?

NICHOLAS. It's a very useful one, at any rate.

SQUEERS. I believe you. Graymarsh, what's a horse?

GRAYMARSH. A beast, sir.

SQUEERS. So it is. A horse is a quadroped, and quadroped's Latin for beast, as anybody that's gone through the grammar knows, or else where's the use in having grammars at all?

NICHOLAS. Where indeed.

SQUEERS. (*To Graymarsh.*) And as you're so perfect in that, go to *my* horse, and rub him down well, or I'll rub *you* down. The rest go and draw water up till somebody tells you to leave off, for it's washing day tomorrow, and they'll want the coppers filled. (*The boys hurry out, Mobbs and Bolder hurrying more than the others.*) Except—for Mobbs and Bolder. (*Everyone stops. Some of the boys push Mobbs and Bolder forward, towards Squeers. Then the others go out, as Mrs. Squeers and Wackford go too. Smike tries to go as well.*) Stay there, Smike. They'll need taking to their beds. (*He turns to Nicholas.*) This is the way we do it, Nickleby. (*Squeers lifts his cane. Blackout. Some of the older men of the company appear in a little light. As they speak this narration, we see Nicholas sit morosely down at the side of the stage. Squeers, Smike, Mobbs, and Bolder have gone.*)

NARRATORS.

And Nicholas sat down, so depressed and self-degraded that if death could have come upon then he would have been happy to meet it.

The cruelty of which he had been an unwilling witness,

The coarse and ruffianly behaviour of Squeers,

The filthy place,

The sights and sounds about him,

All contributed to this feeling.

And when he recollected that, being there as an assistant, he was the aider and abetter of a system which filled him with disgust and indignation,

He loathed himself. (*Blackout.*)

Scene Eleven

Bare stage. Outside Dotheboys Hall. Enter Mrs. Squeers,

47

and, from the other side, her 20-year old daughter Fanny.

FANNY. Mama! Mama, I'm home!
MRS. SQUEERS. Fanny. (*Enter Fanny's friend Tilda Price, followed by her swain John Browdie, carrying luggage.*)
FANNY. Tilda Price brought me home, mama.
MRS. SQUEERS. Miss Price.
TILDA. (*A little bob.*) Good morning, ma'am.
JOHN. Ah, 'allo, missus. How's thissen?
FANNY. And John as well.
MRS. SQUEERS. I see.
FANNY. (*Aside to Mrs. Squeers.*) Mama, do ask them in.
MRS. SQUEERS. Hm. Would you care for a glass of something, Miss Price? (*Slight pause.*) Mr. Browdie?
JOHN. Ay. We would that, certainly.
MRS. SQUEERS. Well, then—
JOHN. As soon as tied me 'orse. (*John goes out to tie his 'orse. Fanny confidentially to Mrs. Squeers.*)
FANNY. Engaged.
MRS. SQUEERS. Who is?
FANNY. She is.
MRS. SQUEERS. To who?
FANNY. To him.
MRS. SQUEERS. At her age? (*Pause.*) Well, I suppose, she is quite easy on the eye.
FANNY. And, after all, he's hardly what you'd call a gentleman. (*Re-enter John.*)
JOHN. Right then. Let's have that glass of summat, missus, and let's have it sharpish, eh? (*He and Tilda go out, as:*)
FANNY. (*To Mrs. Squeers.*) No. Certainly. Not what you'd call a gentleman, at all. (*Fanny and Mrs. Squeers follow out John and Tilda.*)

Scene Twelve

The Boys drag on a sofa to represent the Squeers' parlour. Squeers is drinking, Mrs. Squeers is trying Belling's clothes on young Wackford. Phib is in attendance.

SQUEERS. Well, my dear, so what do you think of him?

MRS. SQUEERS. Think of who? (*Fanny comes in, having just said her goodbyes to Tilda and John. She sits, knits, and listens, as:*)

SQUEERS. The new man.

MRS. SQUEERS. Oh. Young Knuckleboy.

SQUEERS. Young Nickleby.

MRS. SQUEERS. Well, if you want to know, Squeers, I'll tell you that I think him quite the proudest, haughtiest, turned-up nosediest—

SQUEERS. He is quite cheap, my dear. In fact, he's very cheap.

MRS. SQUEERS. I don't see why we need another man at all.

SQUEERS. Because it says in the advertisement quite clearly—

MRS. SQUEERS. Fiddlesticks it *says*. You *say,* in the advertisement, it's "Education by Mr. Wackford Squeers and his able assistants", but that don't mean you have to have 'em, does it? Sometimes, Squeers, you try my patience.

SQUEERS. Sometimes, you try mine.

MRS. SQUEERS. What's that?

SQUEERS. Well, my love, any slave-driver in the West Indies is allowed a man under him, to see his blacks don't run away, or get up a rebellion; and I want a man under me, to do the same with our blacks, till such time as little Wackford is able to take charge.

WACKFORD. Oh, am I?

MRS. SQUEERS. (*Impatiently.*) Am you what?

WACKFORD. Oh, am I to take charge of the school when I grow up father?

SQUEERS. Yes, of course you are.

WACKFORD. Oh. Oh. Oh, won't I give it to 'em. Won't I make 'em shriek and squeal and scream. (*The Squeerses look at each other. This exemplary attitude on the part of their son has brought them back together.*)

SQUEERS. Of course you will, my boy, of course you will.

FANNY. (*Unable to keep silence.*) Papa... (*Squeers and Mrs. Squeers look at Fanny.*) Who is this—person? This young man?

MRS. SQUEERS. (*Impatient again.*) Oh, he's the new assistant, and your father has got some nonsense in his head he's the son of a gentleman that died the other day.

FANNY. A gentleman.

MRS. SQUEERS. Yes, but I don't believe a word of it. If he's a gentleman's son at all, he's a fondling, that's my opinion.

SQUEERS. Foundling, and he's nothing of the kind. His father was married, *to* his mother years before he was born, and she's alive now.

MRS. SQUEERS. Well, all I say—

SQUEERS. (*Stands.*) And if you do dislike him, dear, I don't know anyone shows dislike better than you do, and if there's a touch of pride about him, then I do not believe there is a woman living that can bring a person's spirit down as quick as you.

MRS. SQUEERS. Oh, is that so.

SQUEERS. My love. (*Pause. Mrs. Squeers looks at Squeers. Then she laughs. Squeers laughs too.*)

MRS. SQUEERS. Come, Wackford. (*Mrs. Squeers, still laughing, gestures Wackford to follow her, and goes out. Squeers, laughing too, goes out. Fanny and Phib left.*)

FANNY. Well? So what's he like?

PHIB. He's lovely.

Scene Thirteen

The Boys take out the sofa and some lie down, to represent the common dormitory. Smike is sitting. Nicholas, still sitting at the side of the stage, now stands, and goes to Smike. Nicholas carries a book.

NICHOLAS. Hallo. (*Smike looks up, scared, and flinches a little.*) Please, don't be frightened. (*Nicholas crouches down near Smike. He puts down his book.*) Are you cold? (*Smike shakes his head.*) You're shivering. (*Pause. Nicholas stands to go. He stops when Smike speaks.*)

SMIKE. Oh, dear. (*Nicholas turns back.*) Oh, dear, oh, dear. My heart. Will break. It will. (*Louder, more forceful.*) It *will*.

50

I know it *will.*

NICHOLAS. (*Embarrassed, looking round.*) Shh, shh.

SMIKE. Remember Dorker, do you?

NICHOLAS. Dorker?

SMIKE. I was with him at the end, he asked for me. Who will I ask for? Who? (*Pause. Nicholas doesn't know what Smike is talking about.*)

NICHOLAS. Who will you ask for when? (*Smike back into himself again.*)

SMIKE. No One. No Hope. Hope Less. (*Slight pause.*)

NICHOLAS. (*Feebly.*) There's always hope.

SMIKE. (*To himself.*) Is there? (*Smike turns again to Nicholas. Forcefully.*) O-U-T-C-A-S-T. A noun. Substantive. Person cast out or rejected. Abject. And foresaken. Homeless. Me. (*Nicholas looks at Smike. He doesn't know what to say. Pause. Then Fanny enters, behind Nicholas. She takes in the scene.*)

FANNY. Oh—I'm sorry. (*Nicholas turns.*) I was looking for my father.

NICHOLAS. He's not here.

FANNY. I see. (*Pause.*) I beg your pardon, sir. How very awkward.

NICHOLAS. Please, please don't apologise.

FANNY. I thank you, sir. Oh...Sir. (*Fanny curtseys, turns, turns back, turns again and goes. Nicholas to go out too, when he realises he's left his book. He looks back to Smike, who has picked up the book and is holding it to himself. Nicholas decides to leave Smike with the book. Smike is left alone, with the sleeping boys. Blackout.*)

Scene Fourteen

Miss La Creevy's house in the Strand. Enter Kate and Hannah, with luggage, from upstage.

HANNAH. Is it the East End that you're going to, Miss?

KATE. That's right. Is that unusual, as a place to live?

HANNAH. (*Trying to avoid answering "yes."*) Well, uh... (*Enter Mrs. Nickleby and Miss La Creevy.*)

MISS LA CREEVY. Well, I'm still afraid that millinery is not a healthly occupation, for your dear Kate or anyone else. For I remember getting three young milliners to sit for me, and they were all very pale and sickly.

MRS. NICKLEBY. Oh, Miss La Creevy, that's not a general rule by any means. For I recall employing one to make a scarlet cloak, at the time when scarlet cloaks were fashionable, and she had a very red face—a very red face indeed.

MISS LA CREEVY. Perhaps she drank.

MRS. NICKLEBY. Well, I don't know how that may have been, but I do know she had an extremely red face, so your argument goes for nothing. (*Pause.*) And Kate, who knows, if you work well, you might be taken into partnership with Madame Mantalini. (*Pause.*) Think. Nickleby and Mantalini. How well it would sound. And, who knows, Dr. Nickleby, the headmaster of Westminister School, living in the same street... (*Slight pause.*) It's not impossible, at all. (*Enter Hannah, followed by Newman Noggs.*)

HANNAH. Uh—it's a gentleman. I think. (*Miss La Creevy looks peevishly at Hannah.*)

NOGGS. Name's Noggs. From Mr. Nickleby. To Thames Street.

KATE. Yes. We'll need a coach, I fear.

NOGGS. I'll get one.

MRS. NICKLEBY. Uh, Mr. Noggs... did not we see you on the morning when my son departed on the coach for Yorkshire?

NOGGS. Me? Oh, no.

MRS. NICKLEBY. I'm sure of it, I—

NOGGS. No. First time I've been out, three weeks. I've had the gout. You ready?

KATE. Yes. (*She turns to Miss La Creevy.*) We are sorry, very sorry, to leave you, Miss La Creevy.

MISS LA CREEVY. Oh, that's stuff. You cannot shake me off that easily. I'll see you very often, come and call, and hear how you get on. (*Kate smiles.*) And if, in all the world, there's no-one else to take an interest in your welfare, there will still be one poor, lonely heart that prays for it night and day.

NOGGS. Uh—can we go? (*And the Nicklebys leave with Mr. Noggs, Miss La Creevy and Hannah waving, the former with a handkerchief pressed to her nose.*)

Scene Fifteen

The parlour at Dotheboys Hall. Early evening. Enter Tilda and Fanny, both dressed up to the nines. Phib enters, too, setting the table with tea and a plate of bread and butter.

TILDA. Engaged!

FANNY. No, not exactly. Not exactly, as it were, engaged. But going to be, there is no question. (*They sit on the sofa.*)

TILDA. Fanny, that is *wonderful.*

FANNY. Because, you see, his very presence, coming here to live with us, beneath this roof, and under the most mysterious circumstances...

TILDA. Fanny, what's he said? (*Slight pause.*)

FANNY. What do you mean?

TILDA. I mean—what has he *said?* (*Pause.*)

FANNY. Don't ask me what he said, my dear. If you had only seen his look...

TILDA. Was it like this? (*Tilda gives a love-lorn look.*)

FANNY. Like that?

TILDA. John looked at me like that.

FANNY. Well, so did he. Like that, entirely, only rather more genteel.

TILDA. Well, then, that's it.

FANNY. That's what?

TILDA. He must mean something, if he looks like that. He must feel... something very strong.

FANNY. Oh, I'm so jealous of you, Tilda!

TILDA. Why?

FANNY. Because you are so fortunate. That your mama and papa are so readily agreeable to your engagement, indeed appear not to have thought twice about it, whereas my mother

53

and my father are so bitterly opposed to my dear Nicholas; and will throw all kinds of obstacles in our way; and will force us to meet in secret, and deny our passion...Oh that my course of love were half as simple, quiet and smooth as yours! (*Pause.*)

TILDA. I cannot wait to see him.

FANNY. Oh, I'm shaking!

TILDA. Yes, I know just how you feel. (*Knock, knock.*)

FANNY. Oh, there he is! Oh, Tilda!

TILDA. Shh. Just say, come in.

FANNY. (*Almost silently.*) Come in! (*Tilda a glance at Phib, who looks away. Nothing.*)

TILDA. Come in! (*Nicholas comes in.*)

NICHOLAS. Good evening. I understood from Mr. Squeers that—

FANNY. Oh, yes. It's all right. Father's been called away, but you won't mind that, I dare venture.

NICHOLAS. (*Out front.*) And Nicholas opened his eyes at this, but he turned the matter off very coolly—not minding particularly about anything just then—and went through the ceremony of introduction to the miller's daughter with as much grace as he could muster. (*Bowing to Tilda.*) Your servant, ma'am.

FANNY. We are only waiting for one more gentleman.

NICHOLAS. (*Out front.*) It was a matter of equal moment to Nicholas whether they were waiting for one gentleman or twenty; and being out of spirits, and not seeing any especial reason why he should make himself agreeable, looked out of the window and sighed. (*He looks "out of the window" and sighs.*)

TILDA. Oh, Mr. Nickleby.

NICHOLAS. (*With a start.*) I'm sorry.

TILDA. Please, don't apologise. Perhaps your langour is occasioned by my presence. But, please, don't heed me. You may behave just as you would if you two were alone.

FANNY. (*Blushing.*) Tilda! I'm ashamed of you! (*The young women giggle.*)

NICHOLAS. And here the two friends burst into a verity of giggles, glancing from time to time at Nicholas, who, in a state of unmixed astonishment, gradually fell into one of irrepressible amusement.

TILDA. Come, now, Mr. Nickleby. Will you have tea?

54

NICHOLAS. (*Cheerfully, going over to sit.*) Oh, certainly. I'm
honoured. And delighted. (*The women look at each other. Tilda
a little nod, Fanny a deep breath.*)
FANNY. Some—bread-and-butter?
NICHOLAS. Please. (*Nicholas being poured tea and helping him-
self to bread-and-butter when there's another knock. Tilda stands,
Fanny gestures to Phib, who admits John Browdie, looking
scrubbed and uncomfortable in a huge collar and white waist-
coat.*)
TILDA. Well, John.
JOHN. Well, lass.
FANNY. I beg your pardon, Mr. Nickleby—Mr. John Browdie.
JOHN. Your servant, sir.
NICHOLAS. Yours to command, sir.
FANNY. Please, Mr. Browdie, sit down. (*John, as he sits.*)
JOHN. Old woman gone awa, be she?
FANNY. She has.
JOHN. (*Helping himself to bread-and-butter.*) And schoolmaster
as well?
FANNY. Yes, yes.
JOHN. An' just the four o' us?
FANNY. That's right. Do have some bread-and-butter. (*John,
in mid-bite, grins hugely. Then, to Nicholas.*)
JOHN. Tha won't get brea-and-butter ev'ry night, eh, man?
(*Nicholas a weak smile.*) In fact, I tell thee, if tha stay here
long enough, tha'll end up nowt but skin and bone. (*John laughs
hugely. Nicholas annoyed by this criticism of his employer. John
elbows Fanny.*) Just skin and bone, eh, Fanny? (*John looks
back to Nicholas. To explain.*) I tell tha, man, last teacher,
'ad 'ere, when turned sideway, couldn't tell were there! (*Nicholas suddenly to his feet.*)
NICHOLAS. Sir, I don't know whether your perceptions are quite
keen enough, to enable you to understand that your remarks
are highly offensive, to me and my employer, but if they are,
please have the goodness to— (*Tilda stops John's response.*)
TILDA. If you say one more word, John, only half a word, I'll
never speak to you again.
JOHN. Oh. Weel. I'll shut me mouth, then. Eh? (*John eats bread-*

and-butter and slurps his tea. Fanny, overcome, stands and runs to the side. Tilda follows. Nicholas looks alarmed.)

TILDA. Fanny, what's the matter?

FANNY. Nothing.

TILDA. There was never any danger of an altercation, was there, Mr. Nickleby?

NICHOLAS. *(A step towards the women.)* No, none at all. *(Tilda to Nicholas, Fanny still sniffing.)*

TILDA. Say something kind to her.

NICHOLAS. Why, what—

TILDA. Or better, why don't John and I go off next door, and leave you two together? For a little while.

NICHOLAS. Whatever for?

TILDA. Whatever for? And her dressed up so beautifully, and looking really almost handsome. I'm ashamed of you.

NICHOLAS. My dear girl, what is it to me how she is dressed, or how she looks? It's hardly my concern. *(Tilda quickly to the table.)*

TILDA. Don't call me a dear girl, or Fanny will be saying it's my fault. We will play cards. Phib, dear, please clear the table. *(Phib clears the table, Tilda whispers to Fanny, and John finishes the bread-and-butter, as Nicholas speaks out front.)*

NICHOLAS. And all of this was completely unintelligible to Nicholas, who had no other distinct impression, than that Miss Squeers was an ordinary-looking girl, and her friend Miss Price a pretty one, and that he had been called to join in a game of Speculation. *(Fanny and Tilda both standing near the chair opposite John.)*

TILDA. So, who's to partner whom?

NICHOLAS. *(Obviously, moving to a chair opposite an empty chair.)* I'll partner you, Miss Price.

TILDA. Oh, *sir.*

NICHOLAS. *(Taking this response as meaning assent.)* It will be my great pleasure. *(Tilda glances at Fanny, and sits opposite the chair beside which Nicholas is standing. Fanny sits opposite John. Nicholas tearing up cards for chips.)*

FANNY. *(Hysterically.)* Well, Mr. Browdie, it appears we're to be partners.

JOHN. *(Dumbfounded.)* Aye.

NICHOLAS. I'll deal?

FANNY. Oh, please, do deal. (*Nicholas deals five cards to each player. They look at their cards.*) Well, Mr. Browdie?

JOHN. (*Pushing two chips into the centre.*) Two on spades.

NICHOLAS. Miss Price?

TILDA. (*Three chips.*) Bid three. On hearts.

FANNY. (*Putting one chip in.*) I'll—pass.

NICHOLAS. (*Putting one chip in.*) Then hearts it is. (*Fanny a sharp intake of breath. The hand is played out in total silence. The principle is the same as whist, with each player laying a card for each trick, hearts being trumps. Tilda and Nicholas win.*) Well, then. We've won.

FANNY. And Tilda something that she'd not expected to win, I think.

TILDA. (*Ingenuously.*) Oh, only seven, dear. (*John dealing another hand.*)

FANNY. (*To Tilda.*) How dull you are.

TILDA. Oh, no, indeed. I am in excellent spirits. It was thinking *you* seemed out of sorts.

FANNY. Oh, me? Why, no.

TILDA. Your hair's coming out of curl, dear.

FANNY. Pray, dear, don't mind me. You'd better attend to your partner.

NICHOLAS. Thank you for reminding her. She had. (*John looking black.*)

TILDA. One diamond.

FANNY. Two clubs.

NICHOLAS. Two diamonds.

JOHN. Three clubs.

TILDA. Pass.

FANNY. Pass.

NICHOLAS. Pass. (*John looks round. Nicholas and Tilda indicate they have no further bid. The hand is played, and, surprisingly, Nicholas and Tilda win again, on the last trick, with Nicholas's king of clubs. Nicholas pulls in the chips. Tilda deals again during:*)

TILDA. Well, I never had such luck. It's all you, Mr. Nickleby, I'm sure. I should like to have you for a partner always.

NICHOLAS. Well, I wish you had.

TILDA. Though if you win at cards, of course, you'll have a bad wife, sure as sure.

NICHOLAS. Not if your wish is gratified, Miss Price. (*He picks up his cards. Aware of the silence of the others.*) We have all the talking to ourselves, it seems.

FANNY. Oh, but you do it so well, Mr. Nickleby. It would be quite an outrage to interrupt you, wouldn't it? Two hearts.

NICHOLAS. Pass. (*Pause.*)

TILDA. John, dear, your bid.

JOHN. My what?

TILDA. Your bid.

JOHN. (*Throwing down his cards.*) Well, damn me if I'm going to take this longer. (*Pause. The young women very shocked.*)

NICHOLAS. Erm...

JOHN. (*Stands.*) And you are coming home with me, now, Tilda, and him o'ert there can look sharp for a broken head next time he comes near me.

TILDA. Mercy on us, what is all this?

JOHN. Home! Home, now, home! (*Fanny crying.*)

TILDA. And here's Fanny in tears, now. What can be the matter?

FANNY. Oh, don't you bother, ma'am. Oh, don't you trouble to enquire.

TILDA. Well, you are monstrous polite, ma'am.

FANNY. Well, I shall not come to you to take lessons in the art, ma'am.

TILDA. And you need not take the trouble to make yourself plainer than you are, ma'am, because it's quite unnecessary.

FANNY. Oh! Oh, I can thank God that I haven't the boldness of some people!

TILDA. (*Standing.*) And I can thank God I haven't the envy of others. While wishing you a good night, ma'am, and pleasant dreams attend your sleep.

FANNY. Tilda, I hate you! (*Tilda sweeps out, followed by John, with a dark look at Nicholas. Fanny, weeping, thumps Phib. Nicholas, out front:*)

NICHOLAS. This is one consequence, thought Nicholas, of my cursed readiness to adapt myself to any society into which chance carries me. If I had sat mute and motionless, as I might have

58

done, this would not have happened. (*Pause. End of reportage. Nicholas flails.*) What did I do? What did I do? (*Nicholas withdraws.*)

FANNY. Oh, I swear that there is no-one in the world more miserable than I. And never has been. And never will be. (*Pause.*)

PHIB. (*Carefully.*) Well, I can't help saying, miss, if you were to kill me for it, that I never saw anyone look so vulgar as Miss Price this night.

FANNY. Oh, Phib, how you do talk. (*Pause.*)

PHIB. And I know it's very wrong of me to say so, Miss, Miss Price being a friend of yours and all, but she do dress herself out so, and go on in such a manner to get noticed: well, if people only saw themselves.

FANNY. Now, Phib, you know you mustn't talk like that.

PHIB. So vain. And so, so plain.

FANNY. And I will hear no more of this. It's true, Miss Price has faults, has many, but I wish her well. And above all, I wish her married. And I think it desirable—most desirable, from the nature of her failings—that she is married as soon as possible.

PHIB. Yes, miss. (*A knock.*)

FANNY. Who's that? Come in. (*Enter Tilda. Phib exit.*)

TILDA. Well, Fanny. (*Slight pause.*) Well, Fanny, you see I have come back to see you. Although we had bad words.

FANNY. I bear no malice, Tilda. I am above it.

TILDA. Don't be cross, please, Fanny. I have come to tell you something.

FANNY. What may that be, Tilda?

TILDA. Well... Well, this. After we left here, John and I had the most dreadful quarrel. But after a great deal of wrangling, and saying we would never speak again, we made it up, and John has promised that first thing tomorrow morning he'll put our names down in the church, and I give you notice to get your bridesmaid's frock made now. There!

FANNY. Oh, *Tilda.* Oh, dear Tilda. (*And the two women burst into tears and embrace each other.*) Oh, I'm so *happy.* (*Tilda decides to strike while the iron is cool.*)

TILDA. But, now, Fanny, there's the matter of young Mr. Nickleby.

FANNY. Oh, him. He's nothing to me.

59

TILDA. Oh, come, now, Fanny, that's not true.

FANNY. It Is. I hate him. And I wish that he was dead. And me as well.

TILDA. Now, dear. You know you'll think very differently in five minutes, and wouldn't it be much nicer to take him back in favour?

FANNY. Oh, Tilda. How could you have acted so mean and dishonourable. I wouldn't have believed it of you.

TILDA. Now, Fanny, you're talking as if I murdered someone.

FANNY. Very near as bad.

TILDA. Oh, don't be silly. It's not my fault I've got enough good looks to make some people civil. Persons don't make their own faces, and it's no more my fault if mine is a good one than it is other people's fault if their's is not.

FANNY. (*In horror.*) Oh, *Tilda.*

TILDA. Fanny, I don't mean—

FANNY. Now, go. Go back home at once.

TILDA. Oh, Fanny—

FANNY. Now, at once, d'you hear me?

TILDA. Very well, but—

FANNY. NOW. (*Fanny turns firmly away. Tilda to the exit. She turns back. Fanny turns slowly to Tilda. Tilda gives a little, shruggy, affectionate gesture, as if to apologise. Pause. Then Fanny runs to her friend, crying.*) Oh, I'm so *happy* for you, Tilda.

Scene Sixteen

The Boys clear the Dotheboys Hall furniture and set two meagre, broken chairs and a threadbare carpet. The Nicklebys' new house in Thames St. Mrs. Nickleby, Kate and Noggs—who carries their luggage—enter during the narration.

NARRATION.
And at that very moment, Kate and Mrs. Nickleby arrived at their new home.

Around, the squalid slums of the East End of London—

And behind, a wharf that opened to the river—

And nearby, an empty kennel, and some bones of animals—

Past which they quickly walked,

And went inside.

NOGGS. (*Putting down the luggage.*) Well, here it is.
KATE. I see.
NOGGS. It's not, of course... There are some bits of furniture.
And there's a fire made up. I'm sure, although it looks a little
gloomy, it can be made, quite...
KATE. Yes. (*Pause.*)
MRS. NICKLEBY. Well, well, my dear. Is it not thoughtful and
considerate of your kind uncle? To provide us with...
NOGGS. Your uncle, yes. (*Noggs picks up the luggage and takes
it to another room in the house.*)
KATE. Oh, mama, this house is so depressing. I—one could im-
agine that some dreadful—that some awful thing had—
MRS. NICKLEBY. Lord, dear Kate, don't talk like that, you'll
frighten me to death.
KATE. It's just a foolish fancy.
MRS. NICKLEBY. Well, Kate, I'll thank you to keep your foolish
fancies to yourself, and not wake up my foolish fancies to keep
them company.
KATE. Yes, I'm sorry. (*The two women look at each other.
Then, quite suddenly, they embrace. Noggs enters.*) Mr. Noggs,
we need detain you no longer.
NOGGS. Is there nothing more?
KATE. No, nothing, really. Thank you.
MRS. NICKLEBY. (*Fumbling in her purse.*) Perhaps, dear, Mr.
Noggs would like to drink our healths.
KATE. I think, mama, you'd hurt his feelings if you offered
it. (*Noggs bows and withdraws. The women sit.*)
NARRATION.
Gloomy and black in truth the old house was—

No life was stirring there—

And everything said coldness, silence and decay.

Scene Seventeen

Outside Dotheboys' Hall. Day. Enter Nicholas.

NICHOLAS. And so it happened that, the next day, during the short daily interval that was suffered to elapse between what was pleasantly called the dinner of Mr. Squeers' pupils and their return to the pursuit of useful knowledge, Nicholas was engaged in a melancholy walk, and brood, and listless saunter. (*Nicholas perambulates as Tilda and Fanny enter, arm-in-arm.*)

TILDA. And Miss Price, who had stayed the night with Miss Squeers, was at that same being taken by her best friend at least as far home as the second turning of the road.

FANNY. (*Seeing Nicholas.*) Ah! Him!

TILDA. Oh, Fanny, shall we turn back? He hasn't seen us yet.

FANNY. No, Tilda... It is my duty to go through with it, and so I shall. (*Nicholas walks straight past Tilda and Fanny.*)

NICHOLAS. (*As he passes.*) Good morning.

FANNY. (*Nudging Tilda violently.*) He's going. I shall faint.

TILDA. Oh, Mr. Nickleby, come back!

FANNY. (*Staggering slightly, and needing to be supported by Tilda.*) I know I shall—

TILDA. Oh, Mr. Nickleby— (*Nicholas turns back, and comes to Tilda and Fanny.*)

NICHOLAS. Um, what's the—

TILDA. Just, please, help— (*Nicholas to hold Fanny, when that young lady expertly twists and falls backwards into his arms. For a moment, they stand there, and then Nicholas, unable to prevent himself, falls over backwards, Fanny on top of him.*)

NICHOLAS. Miss Squeers...

FANNY. (*Coming around.*) Oh, dear, this foolish faintness—

TILDA. It's not foolish, dear. You have no reason to feel shamed.

It's others, who provoke it, who should—

NICHOLAS. Ah. I understand. (*Nicholas manhandles Fanny to a sitting position.*) You are still resolved to fix it upon me. I see. Although I told you last night it was not my fault.

TILDA. There, he says it was not his fault. Perhaps you were too jealous, or too hasty with him? He says it was not his fault. I think that is apology enough.

NICHOLAS. Um—

FANNY. All right, Tilda. You've convinced me. I forgive him. (*Fanny lies back on Nicholas again.*)

NICHOLAS. Oh, dear. This is more serious than I supposed. Allow me— (*He dislodges Fanny, and stands. Fanny stands with Tilda.*) May I speak? (*The two women look at him with eager anticipation.*) I must say—that I am very sorry—truly and sincerely so—for having been the cause of any difference among you last night. I reproach myself most bitterly for having been so unfortunate as to cause the dissention that occured, although I did so, I assure you, most unwittingly and heedlessly. (*Pause.*)

TILDA. Well, that's not all you have to say, surely.

NICHOLAS. No, it is not, I fear there is something more. (*Slight pause.*) It is a most awkward thing to say, as the very mention of such a supposition makes one look like a puppy—but, still... May I ask if that lady supposes that I entertain...a sort of... (*Quickly.*) Does she think that I'm in love with her?

FANNY. Oh! (*Change of tack.*) Oh, answer for me, dear.

TILDA. Of course she does.

NICHOLAS. She does?

TILDA. Of course.

FANNY. And you may say, dear Tilda, that if Mr. Nickleby had doubted that, he may set his mind at rest. His sentiments are completely recipro—

NICHOLAS. Stop!

FANNY. Whatever for?

NICHOLAS. Pray hear me. This is the grossest and wildest delusion, the completest and most signal mistake, that ever human being laboured under or committed. I have scarcely seen the young lady half a dozen times, but if I had seen her sixty times, or sixty thousand, it would be and will be precisely the same.

63

I have not one thought, wish, or hope, connected with her unless it be—and I say this, not to hurt her feelings, but to impress her with the real state of my own—unless it be the one object dear to my heart as life itself, of being one day able to turn my back on this accursed place, never to set foot in it again or to think of it—even think of it—except with loathing and disgust. (*Pause. Then Nicholas, out front.*) And with this particularly plain and straightforward declaration, Nicholas bowed slightly, and waiting to hear no more, retreated. (*Nicholas retreats.*)

TILDA. But oh, poor Fanny! Her anger, rage and vexation are not to be described.

FANNY. Refused! (*Fanny starts to push at Tilda, to make her go away, as punishment for encouraging her.*)

TILDA. (*Being pushed, and beginning to enjoy Fanny's fury, and find it amusing.*) Refused by a teacher picked up by advertisement at an annual salary of five pounds payable at indefinite periods... (*Really taunting now.*) ...and this too in the presence of a little chit of a miller's daughter of eighteen,

FANNY. (*Pushing and shoving.*) ...who was going to be married, to a man who had gone down on his very knees to ask her! (*And, with a little, dismissive gesture, Fanny turns, runs to the side and weeps, while Tilda, still laughing, dances out the other way, and Nicholas speaks out front.*)

NICHOLAS. And it may be remarked, that Miss Squeers was of the firm opinion that she was prepossessing and beautiful, and that her father was, after all, master, and Nicholas man, and that her father had saved money and Nicholas had none, all of which seemed to her conclusive arguments why the young man should feel only too honoured by her preference, and all too grateful for her deep affection... (*And Nicholas turns and sees Fanny. She has composed herself now, but this has the effect of making her look even more crumpled. She marches to Nicholas, with an effort at dignity, but then breaks down.*)

FANNY. Sir...I pity you. (*She turns and runs back, as Mrs. Squeers and Smike appear, as if from the house.*) You're right, mama.

MRS. SQUEERS. Right? What about?

FANNY. (*Crying.*) About that Knuckleboy. (*She runs out, as*

64

if into the house.)
MRS. SQUEERS. *(To Nicholas.)* You, sir!
NICHOLAS. Yes, ma'am?
MRS. SQUEERS. You've been wanted in the classroom for ten minutes.
NICHOLAS. Certainly. *(He goes towards Mrs. Squeers, as if into the house.)*
MRS. SQUEERS. Not through the house, sir. Round that way. *(Pause. Then Nicholas turns his collar up against the cold, and goes out another way. Smike makes to follow him.)* Smike! *(Smike turns back to Mrs. Squeers.)* In here. You haven't finished. *(She cuffs Smike on the head as he passes her into the house.)*

Scene Eighteen

The dormitory at Dotheboys Hall. Night. The boys enter and lie down, on the bare stage. Smike enters and sits, with Nicholas' book. Nicholas enters with a candle, to see Smike trying to read the book. Smike can't work out what to do.

SMIKE. Can't do it. With the book. Can't do it, with the book, at all.
NICHOLAS. Oh, please. Don't try. *(Smike crying.)* Don't. For God's sake. I cannot bear it. *(Smike whimpering.)* They are more hard on you, I know. But, please . . .
SMIKE. Except for you, I die.
NICHOLAS. No, no. You'll be better off, I tell you, when I'm gone. *(Smike picks it up after a second.)*
SMIKE. You gone?
NICHOLAS. Shh. Yes.
SMIKE. You going?
NICHOLAS. I was speaking to my thoughts.
SMIKE. *Tell* me. Will you? Will you go? *(Pause.)*
NICHOLAS. I shall be driven to it. Yes. To go away. *(Pause.)*
SMIKE. Please tell me. Is away as bad as here? *(Pause.)*

65

NICHOLAS. Oh, no. Oh, no, there's nothing—
SMIKE. Can I meet you there? Away?
NICHOLAS. Well, yes . . . you can, of course . . .
SMIKE. Can meet you there? Away? And I will find you, in away?
NICHOLAS. You would. And, if you did, I'd try to help you. (*Pause. Nicholas moves away with the candle and sits. He takes out a paper and a pen. He is writing a letter to Kate.*) I miss you terribly, but at least I feel that if my work here prospers— I miss you terribly. (*Pause.*) I took a Latin class today. The boys are—they are not advanced and there is much to do. (*Pause.*) The countryside is— (*Pause. He puts away the letter. He blows out the candle. Darkness.*)

Scene Nineteen

The same. A bell rings offstage, and then cold, morning light. The boys and Nicholas are in the same positions, but, in the blackout, Smike has slipped away.

SQUEERS. (*Off.*) Hey! Hey, you up there? Are you going to sleep all day?
NICHOLAS. We shall be down directly, sir. (*He gestures to the boys, who speed up.*)
SQUEERS. (*Off.*) Well, you'd better be, or I'll be down on some of you in less—Where's Smike? (*Nicholas goes to Smike's place, but sees he isn't there. The boys nearly fully up.*) (*Off.*) I said— where's Smike? (*Nicholas turns and calls.*)
NICHOLAS. He isn't here, sir.
SQUEERS. (*Off.*) What? Not there? (*Pause. Squeers enters, rushes to Smike's place. He sees Smike is absent.*) What does this mean? Where have you hid him?
NICHOLAS. I have not seen him since last night.
SQUEERS. Oh, no? (*Turning to the boys.*) And you? You boys? Have any of you— (*Jennings, who is obscured from Squeers by other boys.*)

66

JENNINGS. Please, sir ...

SQUEERS. Yes? What's that?

JENNINGS. Please, sir, I think he's run away.

SQUEERS. Who said that?

BOYS. Jennings, sir.

SQUEERS. And, where is Jennings?

BOYS. Here, sir. (*Jennings is pushed forward by his fellows. Squeers to Jennings.*)

SQUEERS. So, you think he's run away, do you?

JENNINGS. Yes, sir. Please, sir.

SQUEERS. And what, sir, what reason have you to suppose that any boy would *want* to run away from this establishment? (*Squeers hits Jennings on the face.*) Eh, sir? (*Jennings says nothing. Squeers looks to Nicholas, who is looking away. Squeers to Nicholas.*) And you, Nickleby. I s'pose you think he's run away?

NICHOLAS. I think it's highly likely, yes.

SQUEERS. You do? Perhaps you *know* he's run away?

NICHOLAS. I do not know, sir. And I'm glad I did not, for it would then have been my duty to have warned you.

SQUEERS. Which, no doubt, you would have been devilish sorry to do.

NICHOLAS. I should indeed, sir. (*Mrs. Squeers enters.*)

MRS. SQUEERS. What's going on? Where's Smike?

SQUEERS. He's gone.

MRS. SQUEERS. (*An order, to Squeers.*) Gone? Well, then, we'll find him, stupid. We must search the roads. He hasn't any money, any food. He'll have to beg. He must be on the public road.

SQUEERS. (*Going towards the exit.*) That's true.

MRS. SQUEERS. (*Following.*) And when we catch him, oh ... (*Squeers turns back to the boys. Slowly.*)

SQUEERS. And when we catch him, I will only stop just short of flaying him alive. So, follow your leader, boys, and take your pattern by Smike. If you dare. (*The Squeerses go out. Nicholas and the boys follow.*)

Scene Twenty

The streets of the West End of London. Early morning.
During this opening narration, we set up the breakfast
room of the Mantalinis: a table and two chairs on the
one side, and a single chair on the other. The Narration
is delivered by Kate Nickleby and four or five Milliners.

KATE. It was with a heavy heart, and many sad forebodings,
that Kate Nickleby left the city when its clocks yet wanted a
quarter of an hour of eight, and threaded her way, alone, amid
the noise and bustle of the streets, towards the West End of
London.
MILLINERS.
   At this early hour many sickly girls,

   Whose business, like that of the poor worm, is to produce
   with patient toil the finery that bedecks the thoughtless and
   luxurious,

   Traverse our streets, making towards the scene of their daily
   labour,

   And catching, as if by stealth, in their hurried walk,

   The only gasp of wholesome air and glimpse of sunlight
   which cheers their monotonous existence during the long
   train of hours that make up the working day.

(*The milliners dispersing, as a tall, old footman enters, a little
unsteadily.*)
KATE. Kate saw, in their unhealthy looks and feeble gait, but
too clear an evidence that her misgivings were not wholly ground-
less. (*Kate goes to the Footman, as a male Narrator enters.*)
NARRATOR. She arrived at Madame Mantalini's at the appoin-

ted hour, and was admitted to a small, curtained room, by a tall, elderly footman. (*During the following, Mr. and Madame Mantalini enter to the breakfast table and sit. Madame Mantalini is a handsome, well-dressed middle-aged woman. Her husband wears a morning gown, with a green waistcoat and Turkish trousers, a pink kerchief, bright slippers, black curled whiskers and a moustache. He is younger than his wife.*)

KATE. Excuse me—Mantalini? Are they Italian?

FOOTMAN. Muntle.

KATE. I beg your pardon?

FOOTMAN. Changed his name. From Mr. Muntle. To Mr. Mantalini.

KATE. Oh, I see. (*The footman nods gravely and goes out. Kate sits on the single chair. We gather from the fact that the Mantalinis do not notice her that the room is divided by an imaginary curtain. There is a bad-tempered silence between the Mantalinis, which is broken when Mr. Mantalini speaks.*)

MANTALINI. I tell you again, my soul, that if you will be odiously, demnibly, outrageously jealous, you will make yourself most horrid miserable.

MADAME MANTALINI. (*Pouting.*) I *am* miserable.

MANTALINI. And I tell you, my fastness, that it is a pretty bewitching little countenance you have, but if it is out of humour, it quite spoils itself, and looks very much like a hobgoblin's.

MADAME MANTALINI. It's very easy to talk.

MANTALINI. Not so easy when one is eating an egg and one is provoked into a passion by demned false accusations, my jewel, for the yolk runs down the waistcoat, and yolk of egg don't match it. 'Cept, of course, a yellow waistcoat. Which this ain't. (*Pause. Madame Mantalini breaks.*)

MADAME MANTALINI. You flirted with her all night long.

MANTALINI. No, no, my love.

MADAME MANTALINI. I watched you all the time.

MANTALINI. Oh, bless the little winking eye—was on me all the time?

MADAME MANTALINI. And I say, Mantalini, that you waltz with anyone but me again, I will take poison. I will swear it, now.

MANTALINI. Take poison?

MADAME MANTALINI. Yes.

MANTALINI. You'll take demned poison on account of Mantalini, preciousness?

MADAME MANTALINI. I will.

MANTALINI. He would could have had the hands of a dowager and two countesses—

MADAME MANTALINI. *One* countess.

MANTALINI. (*Stands and goes round to his wife's side of the table.*) But who at a morning concert saw the demndest little fascinator in the world, and married it, and fiddlesticks to every countess in the world?

MADAME MANTALINI. Oh, Mantalini.

MANTALINI. Oh, my little cherub. I'm forgiven?

MADAME MANTALINI. Well...Oh, well.

MANTALINI. (*Moving briskly back to his seat.*) Now, tell me, sapphire, how are we for cash? For there's a horse for sale at Scrubbs, for next to nothing, and if I can raise some discount from Ralph Nickleby, a hundred guineas buys him, mane and crest and legs and tail, all of the demdest beauty. (*Kate looks up in alarm. Madame Mantalini turns her head away.*) Then I can ride him in the park, before the very chariots of the rejected countesses. (*Moving back to his wife.*) My little—princess.

MADAME MANTALINI. Oh, my — Mantalini. (*Kate coughs loudly. Mantalini stands and mimes pulling back the curtain— we hear the swish and rattle from offstage, Mantalini sees Kate.*)

MANTALINI. Well. What's this?

MADAME MANTALINI. Child, who are you?

KATE. (*Standing.*) I—I am sent here, by my uncle. I am sent here for a situation.

MANTALINI. (*Coming closer to Kate.*) And, my dear, you'll have one.

MADAME MANTALINI. Mantalini. (*Kate thrusts Ralph's letter at Madame Mantalini.*)

KATE. There's a letter. From my uncle, Mr. Nickleby.

MADAME MANTALINI. (*Taking the letter, opening it, a little tartly.*) Oh, yes.

MANTALINI. (*Trying to look at the letter.*) Ralph Nickleby?

KATE. I'm sorry, I was—I was left here, by your footman.

70

MANTALINI. What a rascal is that footman, dear. To keep this sweet young creature waiting—

MADAME MANTALINI. (*Folding Ralph's letter.*) Well, dear, I must say that that's your fault.

MANTALINI. My fault, my joy?

MADAME MANTALINI. Of course. What can you expect, dearest, if you will not correct the man? (*Slight pause.*)

MANTALINI. Well, then. Indeed. He shall be horsewhipped.

MADAME MANTALINI. Well, my dear. Your uncle recommends you, and we are, connected with him, in commercial matters. Now, do you speak French?

KATE. Yes, ma'am, I do.

MANTALINI. But do you speak it like a native?

MADAME MANTALINI. (*Ignoring Mr. Mantalini.*) Miss Nickleby, we have twenty young women constantly employed in this establishment.

MANTALINI. Some of them demned handsome, too. (*Mantalini a knowing smirk at Kate. Madame Mantalini clocks it.*)

MADAME MANTALINI. Of whom, I am pleased to say, Mr. Mantalini knows nothing, as he is never in their room, as I will not allow it. (*Mantalini shrugs, poutishly, and lies down on the sofa.*) Now, our hours are from nine to nine, with extra if we're busy, for which there's a little payment, and I'd think your wages would be in the region of five to seven shillings. Is that satisfactory?

KATE. Oh, yes. It's...Certainly.

MANTALINI. Demned satisfactory.

MADAME MANTALINI. Miss Nickleby, you will pay no attention, please, to anything that Mr. Mantalini says.

KATE. I will not, ma'am.

MADAME MANTALINI. So, then, let me take you to the workroom, now, Miss Nickleby. (*Madame Mantalini leads Kate out. Mantalini goes too.*)

Scene Twenty-One

The Mantalinis' workroom, downstage, and the showroom,
upstage. The scene change is performed by Milliners. In the
workroom are clothesrails, tailors' dummies, hatboxes, and
uncompleted dresses and hats. In the showroom are dis-
play tailors' dummies, more hatboxes, a chaise longue
and a tall mirror. For the moment, the showroom is empty,
and the workroom is full of working Milliners, presided
over by a short, bustling, over-dressed lady called Miss
Knag. Madame Mantalini and Kate enter. The Milliners
look Kate up and down, whisper and giggle.

MADAME MANTALINI. Miss Knag?

MISS KNAG. Madame Mantalini.

MADAME MANTALINI. Ah, Miss Knag, this is the young person I spoke to you about.

MISS KNAG. Oh, good morning, miss. (*To the gawping Millin-*
ers.) Come on, come on, no gawping, is there no work to be
done? (*The Milliners set about their tasks with bad humour.*)

MADAME MANTALINI. I think, for the present, it will be better
for Miss Nickleby to come into the showroom with you—

MISS KNAG. Showroom, yes.

MADAME MANTALINI. And try things on for people.

MISS KNAG. People, yes.

MADAME MANTALINI. She'll not be much use yet in any other
way,

MISS KNAG. Way, no.

MADAME MANTALINI. And her appearance will—

MISS KNAG. Suit very well with mine. (*Miss Knag to Kate.*)
For, yes, I see, Miss Nickleby and I are very much a pair—although I am just a little darker, and I have, I think, a slightly
smaller foot. Miss Nickleby will not, I am sure, be too much
offended at my saying that, as our family has always been quite
celebrated for its feet—the smallness of them—ever since the
family had feet at all.

MADAME MANTALINI. You'll take care, Miss Knag, that she understands her hours,

MISS KNAG. Hours,

MADAME MANTALINI. And so forth.

MISS KNAG. So forth, yes.

MADAME MANTALINI. And I'll leave her with you.

MISS KNAG. Yes, of course, dear Madame Mantalini.

MADAME MANTALINI. Good morning, ladies.

EVERYONE. Good morning, madame. (*Madame Mantalini goes out. As she leaves, she finds Mantalini skulking near the doorway. She looks at him, and shakes her head, near tears, and runs off. Mantalini, dramatically, follows.*)

MISS KNAG. Well, what a charming woman.

KATE. Yes. I'm sure she is.

MISS KNAG. And what a charming husband.

KATE. Is he?

MISS KNAG. You don't think so?

KATE. Well—

MISS KNAG. Oh, goodness gracious mercy—where's your taste? And such a dashing man, with such a head of hair and teeth.

KATE. Well, p'raps I'm very foolish—

MISS KNAG. (*With a conspiratorial look at the Milliners.*) Well, I should say you—

KATE. But as my opinion is of very little importance to him or anyone else, I think I shall keep it, just the same. (*Pause. Miss Knag slightly thrown. The odd Milliner, aware of this, giggles. Miss Knag turns to them.*)

MISS KNAG. Well, come on, girls, where are your manners? Make Miss Nickleby welcome. Take her shawl. (*The Milliners bustle round Kate.*)

1st MILLINER. Your shawl, miss?

2nd MILLINER. Can I take your bonnet?

KATE. (*Giving the Milliner her shawl.*) Oh, thank you.

1st MILLINER. Oh, *miss.* And all in black.

KATE. Well, yes, I—

3rd MILLINER. Don't you find it quite intol'r'ble hot? And dustry?

KATE. (*Almost in tears.*) Yes. I do. Oh, yes, I do. (*Embarrassed pause.*)

1st MILLINER. Was it a near relation, Miss?
KATE. My father.
MISS KNAG. (*Calls.*) For what relation?
2nd MILLINER. Father.
MISS KNAG. A long illness, was it?
2nd MILLINER. I don't know.
KATE. Our misfortune was very sudden. Or I might, perhaps, be able to support it better now. (*And the Milliners turn out front.*)
MILLINERS.
And then there came a knock at Madame Mantalini's door,

And there entered a great lady,

Well, a rich one,

Who had come with her daughter for approval of some court dresses,

Long in preparation,

Upon whom Miss Nickleby was told to wait,

(*Madame Mantalini, Miss Knag, Kate, a Rich Lady and her Rich Daughter are in the showroom. The Rich Lady sits on the chaise, the Rich Daughter stands trying on a coat and hat, near the mirror.*)

MADAME MANTALINI. Bonjour, madame.
1st MILLINER. With Miss Knag,
MISS KNAG. Mademoiselle—
3rd MILLINER. And officered of course by—
MILLINERS. Madame Mantalini.
KATE. (*Bustling about with clothes and hats.*) Kate's part in the pageant was humble enough—
MISS KNAG. (*Taking something from Kate.*) La, ma chere—
KATE. Her duties being limited to holding the articles of costume until Miss Knag was ready to try them on...

MISS KNAG. (*Taking something else.*) Ici...

KATE. And now and then tying a string,

MISS KNAG. Or fastening a hook and eye...Merci...

KATE. And thinking that she was beneath the reach of all arrogance and ill-humour.

MISS KNAG. (*Surveying the effect.*) Ah. Mais *oui*.

RICH LADY. (*Off-hand.*) Alors...

MILLINERS.

But as it happened, both the rich lady and her rich daughter were in a terrible temper,

And Miss Nickleby came in for a considerable share of their displeasure.

(*Kate steps backwards from the Rich Daughter, nearly stepping on the foot of the Rich Lady.*)

RICH LADY. She's so awkward.

1st MILLINER. They remarked. (*Kate fumbling, trying to tie a hat on the Rich Daughter.*)

RICH DAUGHTER. Her hands are cold.

2nd MILLINER. They said. (*Kate accidentally pushes the hat forward, so it falls over the Rich Daughter's face.*)

RICH LADY. Can she do nothing right? (*The Rich Daughter takes off the hat, Miss Knag takes her coat, the Daughter and the Rich Lady preparing to go, as:*)

3rd MILLINER. And they wondered how Madame Mantalini could have such girls about her—

MADAME MANTALINI. Madame, je regrette infiniment...

1st MILLINER. And requested they might see some other young person the next time they came...

RICH LADY. Cher Madame, au revoir! (*The Rich Lady and her Rich Daughter sweep out.*)

2nd MILLINER. And so on,

3rd MILLINER. And so forth. (*The Milliners disperse. Kate moves into the workroom area, leaving Madame Mantalini and Miss Knag in the showroom.*)

KATE. And so common an occurrence would hardly be worthy of mention, but for its effect on Kate, who shed many bitter tears when these people were gone, and felt, for the first time, humbled by her occupation. She had, it is true, quailed at the prospect of hard work and drudgery; but she'd felt no degradation in the thought of labour, till she found herself exposed to insolence and pride. (*Kate stays.*)

MISS KNAG. Well, now, Madame Mantalini. That Miss Nickleby is certainly a very creditable young person, indeed.

MADAME MANTALINI. Well, Miss Knag, beyond putting an excellent client out of humour, Miss Nickleby has not done anything very remarkable thus far that I'm aware of.

MISS KNAG. Aware of, no. But, dear Madame, you must make allowances for inexperience. And such.

MADAME MANTALINI. Well, yes, Miss Knag, of course, but in my view she still remains among the awkwardest young girls I ever saw. And not, despite the opinion of her uncle, not that pretty either.

MISS KNAG. Pretty, no. But, Madame Mantalini. That is not her fault, now is it? She should not be blamed for that, and be denied our friendship, should she? (*Slight pause. Madame Mantalini breathes deeply.*)

MADAME MANTALINI. No.

MISS KNAG. No. (*Madame Mantalini goes out. A great beam is spreading across Miss Knag's face, as Kate takes out a letter.*)

KATE. Oh, Nicholas. How happy it makes me to hear from you, in such good spirits. It consoles me so, to think that you at least are comfortable and happy. (*Exit Kate. Miss Knag, quickly.*)

MISS KNAG. I love her. I quite love her. I declare I do.

Scene Twenty-Two

The Dotheboys Hall schoolroom. Bare stage. The boys enter, two of them dragging a pair of steps, the thrashinghorse. They put it centre stage. The boys form two lines either side of it. Nicholas enters, and looks in horror at the thrashing horse. Squeers enters, with a long cane.

76

SQUEERS. Is every boy here? Every boy keep his place. (*Pause.*)
Nickleby, to your place, sir. Coates. Jackson. (*Coates and Jackson go out. Nicholas moves near the thrashing-horse. Mrs. Squeers, Fanny, Young Wackford and Phib enter, and stand to one side. Coates and Jackson re-enter, dragging Smike, who is bound, and filthy, clearly having been caught after spending the night rough. He is brought down to the thrashing-horse.*)
SQUEERS. Untie him, sirs. (*The two boys untie Smike.*) Now, sir, what do you have to say for yourself? (*Pause.*) Nothing, I suppose? (*Pause. Smike glances at Nicholas, who is looking away.*) Well, then. Let's begin.
SMIKE. Oh, spare me, sir.
SQUEERS. What's that?
SMIKE. Oh, spare me, sir.
SQUEERS. Oh, that's all, is it? Well, I'll flog you within an inch of your life, but I will spare you that. (*Pause.*) Coates, Jackson. (*Coates and Jackson help Smike on to a step of the thrashing horse, so that Smike's chin just reaches over the top. Coates and Jackson tie ropes round Smike's hands and the horse, to keep him in place for the flogging.*)
SMIKE. I was driven to it, sir.
SQUEERS. Driven to it? Not your fault, but mine?
MRS. SQUEERS. Hm. That's a good one. (*Squeers goes a little upstage turns, runs, and delivers the first blow. Smike cries out, Squeers grunts. He goes upstage again, runs, and delivers the second blow. He is back upstage again, when Nicholas takes a slight step forward.*)
NICHOLAS. Uh .. This must stop. (*Squeers looks round.*)
SQUEERS. Who said that? Who said stop?
NICHOLAS. I did. I said that it must stop, and stop it will. (*Pause.*) I have tried to intercede. I have begged forgiveness for the boy. You have not listened. You have brought this on yourself.
SQUEERS. (*Dismissively, preparing for his next stroke.*) Get out, Get out. (*Nicholas walks to stand between Squeers and Smike.*)
NICHOLAS. No sir. I can't.
SQUEERS. Can't? You can't? We'll see. (*Squeers walks to

77

Nicholas and strikes his face. Nicholas doesn't respond.) Now leave, sir, and let me to my work. (*Nicholas turns, as if to go, then suddenly turns back, grabs Squeers, pulls him round, and hits him.*) What?

NICHOLAS. You have— (*Squeers tries to hit Nicholas, but Nicholas seizes the cane and beats Squeers with it. During the ensuing, the following things happen: Mrs. Squeers, Wackford and eventually Fanny come to Squeers' aid—somewhat ineffectually: The boys crush round to see, and eventually to obscure, the fight. And Smike, let go, slips away. There is much shouting.*)

MRS. SQUEERS. What do you think you're doing, you madman?

FANNY. Get off him! Get off him, you monster!

WACKFORD. Beastly! Beastly, man! You beast! (*And Nicholas, finished, breaks through the boys and runs out.*)

MRS. SQUEERS. After him! After him, you vermin! Move, run after him! (*The boys, who have no intention of doing anything of the sort, nonetheless disperse, revealing Squeers, sitting on the ground, holding himself.*) Oh, Squeery, Squeery. (*She helps Squeers to his feet.*) Oh, my Squeery. (*Mrs. Squeers takes Squeers out. Wackford and Fanny follow.*)

Scene Twenty-three

In the countryside. Bare stage. Darkness. Nicholas running. John Browdie enters with a lamp. He carries a stout staff.

JOHN. Hey! Hey! Who's that, who's there? Hey! (*John's light reveals Nicholas.*) Eh. It's tha. From school.

NICHOLAS. Yes, I'm afraid so.

JOHN. What's tha mean, afraid?

NICHOLAS. Well, only—

JOHN. Eh, man, what's the matter with thy face?

NICHOLAS. Oh, it's a cut. A blow. But I returned it to the giver, and with interest, too.

JOHN. Nay. Did tha?

NICHOLAS. Yes. For I have been the victim of considerable mistreatment.

JOHN. Eh?

NICHOLAS. At, from the hands of Mr. Squeers. But I have beaten him quite soundly, and am leaving here as a result.

JOHN. Tha what?

NICHOLAS. I said—I've beaten him. (*And John Browdie goes into strange, silent convulsions. It is not immediately clear that he is vastly amused.*) Uh—what ... ?

JOHN. Tha beat the schoolmaster!

NICHOLAS. Yes, I'm afraid—

JOHN. Who ever heard the like!

NICHOLAS. I'm very sorry, but I was—

JOHN. Give me tha hand.

NICHOLAS. Give you my hand?

JOHN. (*Taking Nicholas's hand and pumping it firmly.*) That's right. Give me tha hand. Tha beat the schoolmaster!

NICHOLAS. Yes, I did, and as a consequence—

JOHN. Eh, man, where is tha going?

NICHOLAS. Well, to London ...

JOHN. Has tha owt, in way of cash?

NICHOLAS. Well, no, but as I plan to walk—

JOHN. To walk to Lunnon? Look, man, tha needs cash. At least, for food, and suchlike. (*Finds his purse.*) So, here's money.

NICHOLAS. Oh, I couldn't possibly—

JOHN. Tha couldn't possibly? Tha couldn't possibly without. So, come on, man. At least, accept a soveriegn.

NICHOLAS. Well, I don't know ...

JOHN. And, p'raps, tha'll not use all of it, and send the surplus back, eh? Oh, and take this timber. If tha's walking that far, need this too. (*Nicholas takes the staff. Pause.*) Now, go, be off with thee. (*Pause.*)

NICHOLAS. I cannot thank you, sir, enough. I—after what, the words we had—I cannot—

JOHN. Beat the schoolmaster. I've not heard good as that, for twenty year. (*And John gives Nicholas a big, bear-like hug, and goes out. Nicholas follows.*)

Scene Twenty-four

*The parlour at Dotheboys Hall. Bare stage. Enter Fanny,
furious, clutching a letter she has written. To the audience:*

FANNY. To Mr. Ralph Nickleby. Golden Square. In London.
Sir. My pa requests me to write to you, the doctors considering
it doubtful whether he will ever recover the use of his legs,
which prevents him holding a pen. We are in a state of mind
beyond everything, and my pa is one mask of bruises, both blue
and green...When your nephew, which you recommended for
a teacher, had done this to my pa, and jumped upon his body,
with his feet, and language I will not pollute my pen with describ-
ing, he assaulted my ma with dreadful violence, dashed her
to the earth, and drove her back comb several inches into her
head. A little more and it must have entered her skull. We have
a medical certificate that if it had, the tortoiseshell would have
affected the brain. Me and my brother were then the victims
of his fury; I am screaming out loud all the time I write and
so is my brother which takes off my attention rather, and I
hope will excuse mistakes. The monster, having satiated his
thirst for blood, ran away, taking with him a boy of desperate
character that he had excited to rebellion. I remain yours, and—
cetrer, Fanny Squeers. (*Fanny folds the letter. A knock at the
door.*) Phib! (*Phib enters.*) Someone at the door. P.S: I pity
his ignorance, and despise him. (*Phib goes to the "door". Brooker enters. He is an old man, dressed in rags, and covered in
mud and snow.*)
PHIB. (*Frightened, turning to Fanny.*) Uh...(*Fanny looks at
Brooker. She looks scared, too.*)
BROOKER. (*Takes a step into the room.*) Boy. I've come about
a boy. Lived here. (*Fanny looks at Phib in panic. Phib runs
out. Brooker takes another step into the room.*) My name is
Brooker. Come about a boy. (*Fanny runs out, Brooker following.*)

Scene Twenty-five

Nicholas on his own in the countryside. Bare stage.

NICHOLAS. It's morning. (*Nicholas starts to walk out. Something he hears makes him stop. He turns back. Smike stands there.*) Oh, Smike. Oh—Smike. (*Nicholas quickly to Smike, who falls to his knees.*) Why do you, kneel to me?
SMIKE. To go. Go anywhere. Go everywhere. The world's end. To the churchyard grave. (*Pause.*) I can. You'll let me. Come away with you. (*Pause.*) You are my home. (*Nicholas stands there. He doesn't know what to do. Smike turns his face away. He's crying. Nicholas puts his hand out to Smike. Smike looks back. He sees the hand. Nicholas helps Smike to his feet, and the two of them go slowly out together.*)

END OF ACT ONE.

ACT TWO

Scene One

A group of Narrators on the bare stage. During the following, Noggs enters and sits in his old armchair. A hard-featured, thin-faced man, wearing a dirty nightcap and carrying an unlit candle, is behind him. This man is Mr. Crowl.

NARRATION.

In that quarter of London where Golden Square is situated,

There is a bygone, tumbledown old street,

Two rows of blackened, battered houses,

At the top of one of which there is a meagre garret room;

Where, on a wet and dismal winter's evening,

Newman Noggs,

The clerk to that great man of business Ralph Nickleby,

Sat studying a letter,

Written to his master,

Which had arrived that very afternoon.

NOGGS. (*Reading.*) My pa requests—one mask of bruises—language—thirst for blood. Oh, dear. And cetrer, Fanny Squeers.

Oh, dear, oh, dear. (*Mr. Crowl knocks.*) What's that?

CROWL. (*Unnecessarily loud.*) It's Mr. Crowl. Your Neighbour. Have you got a light?

NOGGS. Oh, yes, do come in, Mr. Crowl.

(*Narrators withdraw as Crowl to Noggs.*)

CROWL. A nasty night, Mr. Noggs.

NOGGS. Oh, does it rain outside?

CROWL. Oh, does it rain? I'm wet through.

NOGGS. (*Looking at his threadbare sleeve.*) Well, it doesn't take much to wet you and me through, does it, Mr. Crowl.

CROWL. Well, but that only makes it more vexatious, doesn't it? (*Pause.*)

NOGGS. You'll forgive me, Mr. Crowl. I must go downstairs to supper.

CROWL. To the Kenwigses?

NOGGS. That's right. It is their wedding anniversary, and Mrs. Kenwigs' uncle is expected, the collector of the water-rate, and I am invited to make up the punch and the numbers. So, you'll let me—

CROWL. Well, now, think of that.

NOGGS. Yes, what?

CROWL. I was invited too.

NOGGS. You were?

CROWL. Indeed I was, but resolved not to go, thinking you were not invited, and planning to spend the evening in your company.

NOGGS. Well, um . . . I was obliged . . .

CROWL. And now, what's there for me to do? (*Pause. Noggs gestures vaguely.*) I know. I've got it. I'll still spend the evening here. And keep your fire up for you. Hm?

NOGGS. Oh . . . very well. (*Noggs turns to go.*)

CROWL. Um, Mr. Noggs, it being such a night . . . Where do you keep your coals?

NOGGS. They're in the coal scuttle. Where coals ought to be. (*Noggs goes out, Crowl pushes out the armchair.*)

CROWL. (*Out front.*) The following, having the misfortune to treat of none but common people, is necessarily of a mean and vulgar character.

Scene Two

The Kenwigs' living room. A small, cluttered room, full of furniture and people. They are the pregnant Mrs. Kenwigs, her eldest daughter Morleena, two other Little Kenwigses—both girls, Mr. and Mrs. Cutler, Miss Green, Mrs. Kenwigs' Sister, a young man called George, a fierce-looking Stout Lady, in a book-muslin dress, and Miss Petowker, an actress. Noggs sits by a small table on which are glasses, trays and a bowl of punch. Mrs. Kenwigs is just greeting him.

MRS. KENWIGS. Dear Mr. Noggs. Now, Miss Petowker, have you met my husband's old friend, George?
GEORGE. I'm most delighted.
MRS. KENWIGS. Miss Petowker's from the Theatre Royal, Drury Lane, and later on she may recite for us.
MISS PETOWKER. Oh, Mrs. Kenwigs... (*Mrs. Kenwigs going to her Sister.*)
GEORGE. Miss Petowker, tell me, how do you fill your days?
SISTER. (*Referring to the Stout Lady.*) My dear, who is that woman?
MRS. KENWIGS. Oh, she's the lady from downstairs.
SISTER. What *does* she think she's wearing?
MRS. KENWIGS. Well, she wouldn't wear it here, but for the fact our supper's cooking on her grate.
SISTER. I see. (*Kenwigs enters, briskly.*)
KENWIGS. Now, Mrs. Kenwigs, if everything's prepared, wouldn't it be best to begin with a round-game?
MRS. KENWIGS. Kenwigs, my dear, I am surprised at you. Would you begin without my uncle?
KENWIGS. Ah. I forgot the collector.
MRS. KENWIGS. (*To Mrs. Cutler.*) He's so particular, that if

84

we begin without him, I shall be out of his will forever.

MRS. CUTLER. Oh, my dear!

MRS. KENWIGS. You have no *notion* how he is. (*To Kenwigs.*) And yet, of course, as good a creature as ever breathed.

KENWIGS. Indeed. The kindest-hearted man that ever was.

GEORGE. It brings the very tears to his eyes, I believe, to be forced to cut the water off when people don't pay.

MRS. KENWIGS. Now, George, if you please.

GEORGE. Oh, I'm sorry. Just my—

MRS. KENWIGS. We'll have none of that.

GEORGE. Was just my little joke.

KENWIGS. Now, George. A joke is a good thing, an excellent thing, but when a joke is made at the expense of Mrs. Kenwigs' feelings I set my face against it. And, even putting Mrs. Kenwigs out of the question—if I *could* put Mrs. Kenwigs out of the question on such an occasion as this—I myself have the honour to be connected with the collector by marriage, and I cannot allow these remarks in my . . . in my apartments. (*Pause.*)

GEORGE. Just my little joke.

KENWIGS. The subject is now closed. (*A ring.*) The bell!

MISS PETOWKER. That's him?

MRS. CUTLER. That's the collector?

STOUT LADY. Who?

MRS. KENWIGS. Yes, yes, it must be, dear Morleena, run straight down and let your uncle in and kiss him most directly when the door is open. Hurry, girl!

MORLEENA. Yes, yes, mama. (*Exit Morleena.*)

MRS. KENWIGS. And, everyone, we must appear to be engaged in light and easy conversation of a general character.

MISS GREEN. Light and easy?

MRS. KENWIGS. Yes, so as to look—

MR. CUTLER. And of a general character?

MRS. KENWIGS. Yes, yes, now Miss Petowker, tell us, if you'd be so kind—

MRS. CUTLER. So as to look—(*Mrs. Kenwigs has turned as sees Mr. Lillyvick, who has been admitted by Morleena.*)

MRS. KENWIGS. Oh, uncle, I'm so pleased to see you.

LILLYVICK. Susan.

MRS. KENWIGS. Oh, so glad.

LILLYVICK. As I, my dear, as I. And may I wish you every happiness. (*Mr. Lillyvick kisses Mrs. Kenwigs.*)

MRS. CUTLER. Well, look at that.

MR. CUTLER. A tax-collector.

MISS GREEN. Kissing.

GEORGE. Actually.

MRS. KENWIGS. And so, uncle, where will you sit?

LILLYVICK. (*Sitting.*) Oh, anywheres, my dear. I'm not particular, at all.

MRS. CUTLER. You hear that?

MR. CUTLER. Anywheres.

MISS GREEN. He's not particular.

GEORGE. At all.

KENWIGS. Um, Mr. Lillyvick, some friends of mine, sir, very anxious for the honour . . .

LILLYVICK. As I am, Kenwigs, just as I am . . .

KENWIGS. Mr. and Mrs. Cutler, Mr. Lillyvick.

MR. CUTLER. I'm proud to know you, sir. As having heard of you so often. In your professional capacity.

KENWIGS. My old friend George you know, I think; of course, Mrs. Kenwigs' sister; Miss Green, who makes up Mrs. Kenwigs' dresses, Mr. Lillyvick; and Mrs. um, downstairs . . . And, Mr. Lillyvick, this here is Miss Petowker of the Theatre Royal Drury Lane, and very glad I am indeed, to make two public characters acquainted.

MISS PETOWKER. I am so pleased to meet you, sir.

LILLYVICK. Yes, yes, most privileged, I'm sure.

KENWIGS. Now, Morleena, where's your sisters, so they can kiss your uncle? (*Morleena pushes forward the two little Kenwigses, and Mr. Lillyvick's attention is reluctantly removed from Miss Petowker so he can kiss them; meanwhile Mrs. Kenwigs is whispered to about Mr. Noggs by her Sister.*)

SISTER. Why doesn't he . . . the threadbare gentleman?

MRS. KENWIGS. Oh, Mr. Noggs, he'd be embarrassed, to be taken notice of. He was a gentleman, you see, before.

LILLYVICK. And where is little Lillyvick?

MRS. KENWIGS. Oh, uncle, in safe hands, in Miss Green's bed, and sleeping like a baby . . .

LILLYVICK. Well, he is a baby.

86

MRS. KENWIGS. Yes, and minded by a girl, of course,

MISS GREEN. Who's being paid nine pence,

MRS. KENWIGS. And thus will see to it no harm befalls your namesake, uncle.

LILLYVICK. Yes, it should be so. (*Pause.*) Well. Susan. Kenwigs. Anniversary.

KENWIGS. Eight years.

LILLYVICK. Eight years. I still recall my niece . . .

STOUT LADY. Recalls his niece?

LILLYVICK. That very afternoon, she first acknowledged to her mother a partiality for Kenwigs. "Mother," she says, 'I love him.'

MRS. KENWIGS. Actually, 'adore him,' I said, uncle.

LILLYVICK. "Love him," you said, Susan, I remember it, and instantly her mother cries out 'what?' and falls at once into convulsions.

MRS. CUTLER. What?

MISS GREEN. Convulsions?

LILLYVICK. Into strong convulsions. For, I'm sure that Kenwigs will forgive me saying so, there was a great objection to him, on the grounds that he was so beneath the family, and would disgrace it. You remember, Kenwigs?

KENWIGS. Certainly.

LILLYVICK. And I, I must confess, I shared that feeling . . . and perhaps it's natural, and perhaps it's not . . .

MRS. CUTLER. Well, I'd say—

STOUT LADY. *Quite* natural.

LILLYVICK. And after they were married, I was the first to say that Kenwigs must be taken notice of. And he *was* taken notice of, because I said so; and I'm bound to say, and proud to say, that I have always found him a most honest, well-behaved and upright sort of man. Kenwigs, shake hands.

KENWIGS. (*Doing so.*) I am proud to do it, sir.

LILLYVICK. And so am I.

KENWIGS. And a very happy life I have led with your niece, sir.

LILLYVICK. And it would have been your own fault if you hadn't, sir.

MRS. KENWIGS. (*Overcome.*) Oh, dear Morleena, kiss your uncle once again.

LILLYVICK. Oh. Well . . .

MRS. KENWIGS. And all of you, dear children, come and kiss your uncle ...

LILLYVICK. Well, indeed, and now to see these three young lively girls ...

MRS. KENWIGS. Oh, yes, oh yes, they are too beautiful.

LILLYVICK. Too beautiful for what, my dear?

MRS. KENWIGS. Too beautiful to live.

MISS GREEN. Oh, Mrs. Kenwigs.... (*Mrs. Kenwigs in tears.*)

MRS. KENWIGS. Oh, far, far too ...

MRS. CUTLER. Oh, dear Mrs. Kenwigs, please ...

SISTER. Oh, come now, Susan, don't distress yourself.

MISS GREEN. Don't give way, dear ...

MRS. KENWIGS. I'm sorry, but I cannot help it, it don't signify. They're just ... they are too beautiful.

KENWIGS. Um, Mrs. Kenwigs, should, perhaps ... While Mr. Noggs makes up the punch, Morleena do her figure dance for Mr. Lillyvick?

MISS GREEN. Oh, yes. It is a spectacle.

MRS. KENWIGS. Oh, no, my dear, it will only worry my uncle.

MISS PETOWKER. Come, I'm sure it won't, now will it, Mr. Lillyvick?

LILLYVICK. I'm sure, dear lady, it is most—

MRS. KENWIGS. (*Recovered.*) Well, then, I'll tell you what. Morleena does the steps, if uncle can persuade Miss Petowker to recite for us afterwards the Blood Drinker's Burial. (*Much applause and encouragement.*)

GEORGE. Oh, yes, indeed.

MISS GREEN. Oh that would be a treat.

STOUT LADY. Blood Drinker's what?

MISS PETOWKER. Oh, now, you know that I dislike doing anything professional at private parties.

MRS. KENWIGS. Oh, but not here? We're all so very friendly and pleasant, that you might as well be going through it in your own room; besides, the occasion ...

MISS PETOWKER. Well ... I can't resist that, Anything in my humble power, I shall be delighted. (*More applause.*)

KENWIGS. Come, then, everyone, form a space here ...

MRS. KENWIGS. Morleena, dear, have you chalked your shoes?

STOUT LADY. She's going to do a poem?

MRS. CUTLER. No, a dance.

MISS PETOWKER. All ready? (*Morleena nods. Some musical accompaniment—from Miss Petowker, humming or otherwise; or perhaps another member of the party. Morleena does her dance—"a very beautiful figure, comprising a great deal of work for the arms," and it is received with unbounded applause. During this, Noggs hands round punch.*)

GEORGE. Bravo!

MRS. CUTLER. Quite wonderful.

MISS GREEN. Oh, Mr. Kenwigs, you must be so proud . . .

MR. CUTLER. Can say with confidence, have never seen the like.

MRS. CUTLER. I wouldn't like to meet her teacher, that's all I can say.

MR. CUTLER. I say, I'd like to shake her teacher by the hand.

KENWIGS. Ah, Noggs, please, the collector first . . .

MRS. KENWIGS. (*To Lillyvick.*) You see, how beautifully she . . . Oh, dear me . . .

MISS PETOWKER. You know—(*Miss Petowker gains attention.*) If I was ever, blessed . . . And if my child were, such a genius as that . . . I'd have her in the opera at once.

KENWIGS. The opera?

MISS PETOWKER. What's wrong?

MRS. KENWIGS. I think that Kenwigs thinks . . . the younger dukes and marquises . . .

LILLYVICK. Yes, very right.

MISS PETOWKER. Oh, sir, one only needs to keep one's pride. I've kept my pride, and never had a thing of that sort. Not a thing.

KENWIGS. Well, then. Perhaps we should give it serious consideration. (*Miss Petowker graciously prepares herself. She whispers to George, and they put out some of the lights to give a better effect.*)

STOUT LADY. What's she doing now? Another dance?

MRS. CUTLER. She's going to recite.

STOUT LADY. What, in the dark?

KENWIGS. Ladies and gentlemen. Pray silence, please, for

Miss Petowker. (*Applause. Miss Petowker strikes an attitude. During this, Crowl enters and goes towards the party.*)

MISS PETOWKER.
'Twas in a back-street tavern that one night it did perchance,
While the wind was howling fiercely, all the bottles were
a-dance,
The candle gutted fitful as they, fearful, drank their ale,
When a dark-eyed stranger entered, bought a drink, and
told a tale.
Oh, he was a—
(*Crowl knocks loudly.*)
What?

MRS. KENWIGS. What's that?

KENWIGS. It sounded like a—

CROWL. It's Mr. Crowl, and Mr. Noggs is wanted.

KENWIGS. (*Admitting Crowl.*) Mr. Noggs?

NOGGS. Who, me?

CROWL. Two people in his room. Both very queer-looking. And covered up with rain and mud.

NOGGS. What, me? By name?

CROWL. By name. (*To Kenwigs.*) The one's a kind of scrawny chap, and not quite right, it seems to me; the other's straighter, darkish, twenty years or so ... (*Miss Petowker shrugs at George, who relights candles. Noggs, who has been going towards the exit, turns back.*)

NOGGS. Dark? Twenty years?

CROWL. Or so. (*Suddenly, Noggs rushes back into the room, grabs a candle, and takes the cup of punch from Mr. Lillyvick.*) Excuse me. Please. (*Noggs rushes out.*) Well, look at that—

MRS. KENWIGS. Well, suppose it should be an express sent up to say his property has all come back again, and the express accounting for the mud and—

KENWIGS. Well, it's not impossible, perhaps, in that case, we should send a little extra punch up—

LILLYVICK. Kenwigs. I'm surprised at you.

KENWIGS. Why, what's the matter, sir?

LILLYVICK. (*Standing*) Why, making such a remark as that, sir. He has had punch already, has he not? My punch, in fact Now, it may well be customary to allow such things here, but

90

it's not the sort of thing I have been used to, when a gentleman is raising up a glass of punch and then another comes and collars it without a 'with your leave' or 'by your leave'...This may be called good manners, but it's not by me, and now it's past my hour to go to bed, and I can find my own way home.

MRS. KENWIGS. Oh, uncle!

KENWIGS. Sir, I'm very sorry, sir.

LILLYVICK. Then it should have been prevented, sir, that's all.

KENWIGS. Well, sir, I didn't...Just a glass of punch, to put you out of temper...

LILLYVICK. Out of temper? Me? Morleena, get my hat.

MISS PETOWKER. (*Bewitchingly.*) Oh, you're not going, sir...

LILLYVICK. I am not wanted here. My hat! (*Morleena, terrified, goes to find Lillyvick's hat.*)

MRS. KENWIGS. Oh, do not speak so, uncle, please...

LILLYVICK. My hat!

KENWIGS. (*Grabbing the hat from Morleena.*) Sir, I must grovel at your feet, and beg you, for your niece's sake, that you'll forgive me.

LILLYVICK. Hm?

KENWIGS. For, for your niece's sake. And little Lillyvick.

LILLYVICK. Well, then. (*Pause.*) Well, then. You are forgiven. (*Applause.*) But let me tell you, Kenwigs, that even if I'd gone away without another word, it would have made no difference respecting that pound or two which I shall leave among your children when I die.

MRS. KENWIGS. Morleena Kenwigs. Now, go down upon your knees, next to your father, and beg Mr. Lillyvick to love you all his life, for he is more an angel than a man, and I have always said so. (*Lillyvick smiles benignly as Morleena, rather uncomfortably, kneels beside her Father.*)

MORLEENA. Uh. Uncle Lillyvick. Uh... (*Suddenly, three high-pitched screams from another room.*)

KENWIGS. What's that?

GEORGE. Where is it?

MRS. KENWIGS. (*To Miss Green.*) Oh, it's your—oh, my baby! (*Mrs. Kenwigs trying to run out, stopped by her sister.*)

91

Oh, my blessed, blessed—
SISTER. Susan, please—
KENWIGS. Now, I will go at once and—
MRS. KENWIGS. Let me go!
KENWIGS. Come, George—
GEORGE. Of course. Where is the—?
MISS GREEN. Up the stairs, just—
MRS. KENWIGS. Oh, my own dear darling, innocent—Oh, let me *go*—
LILLYVICK. What: Little Lillyvick? (*Kenwigs is nearly out of the room, followed by George, when Nicholas bursts into the room, holding little Lillyvick in his arms.*)
KENWIGS. Oh, sir.
LILLYVICK. What's this? Who's this?
NICHOLAS. (*Breathlessly.*) Don't be alarmed. Here is the baby. Safe and sound.
MRS. KENWIGS. (*Rushing to take the baby from Nicholas.*) Oh, oh, my baby . . .
NICHOLAS. It was—a nothing. All that happened was the little girl who watched the baby fell asleep, and the candle set her hair on fire.
MISS GREEN. The wretch! (*Miss Green strides out.*)
NICHOLAS. I heard her cries. And ran down. And the baby was not touched. I promise you.
MISS PETOWKER. Oh, sir, without you, he would certainly have burned to death.
NICHOLAS. Well, no, I'm sure you would have heard it too, and rushed to her assistance. (*Enter Miss Green, pushing a little girl with singed hair.*)
MISS GREEN. Here is the wretch! Look, here she is. Her head all singed.
MRS. CUTLER. And costing ninepence.
MISS GREEN. Which she *won't* receive. Be off with you!
MRS. CUTLER. Yes, off, off, now! (*The poor little girl is pushed out, the little Kenwigses running to catch a glimpse of her singed head before she's gone.*)
LILLYVICK. Now, sir. You have done service, and we must all drink your health.
NICHOLAS. Well, in my absence, I'm afraid, sir. I have had

92

a very tiring journey, and would be most indifferent company. So please forgive me if I go back up to Mr. Noggs. Good night. (*Nicholas goes out.*)

MRS. KENWIGS. That is—the man.

SISTER. And quite delightful.

KENWIGS. Quite uncommonly. Now, don't you think so, Mr. Lillyvick?

LILLYVICK. Well, yes, he is—he seems to be a gentleman.

MISS PETOWKER. Oh, yes... There's something in him, looks, now what's the word?

MISS GREEN. What word?

MISS PETOWKER. You know, when lords and dukes and things go breaking knockers, and playing at coaches, and all that sort of thing?

LILLYVICK. Aristocratic.

MISS PETOWKER. Yes, that's right. That's what he is.

MISS GREEN. Indeed.

KENWIGS. Well, now, perhaps... There is still supper to be had ...

STOUT LADY. Downstairs.

KENWIGS. Downstairs. (*Everyone, going out, as:*)

LILLYVICK. I shall...I should esteem it a great honour, Miss Petowker, soon to hear the ending of your recitation.

MISS PETOWKER. Oh, dear Mr. Lillyvick, you shall. I swear you shall. (*And Mr. Lillyvick takes the arm of Miss Petowker, and leads her into supper.*)

Scene Three

Noggs' garret room. Nicholas and Smike, and Noggs, who has a bottle and two glasses. Nicholas sits in Noggs' chair, reading Fanny Squeers' letter.

NICHOLAS. Monster...boy of desperate character...So, has my uncle yet received this outrageous letter?

NOGGS. Yes, he has—

NICHOLAS. Then, I must go to him at once—

NOGGS. No, no, you mustn't—

NICHOLAS. Mustn't? Why.

NOGGS. Because he hasn't read it yet. And he's, gone away from town. Three days.

NICHOLAS. My mother and sister do not know of this?

NOGGS. They don't.

NICHOLAS. Well, then. At once, I must go to them. Tell me, quick, where are they living? I must go there now.

NOGGS. No, no, you mustn't.

NICHOLAS. Mustn't? Why?

NOGGS. (*Handing glasses to Nicholas and Smike.*) Because ...please, be advised by me. Your uncle—Do not be seen to be tampering with anyone. You do not know this man. And also— (*He pours a drink for each of them. They don't yet drink it.*)

NICHOLAS. Yes? And also?

NOGGS. You come home, after just three weeks. No money, no position. What—what will your mother—

NICHOLAS. Mr. Noggs, I tell you, that three weeks or three hours, if I had stood by—

NOGGS. I know, I know, but still, my dear young man...you can't, you mustn't give way to—this sort of thing will never do, you know, and if you want to get on in the world, if you take the part of everybody that's ill-treated.... (*Suddenly, clapping Nicholas on the arm.*) Damn it, I'm proud of you. I would have done the same myself!

NICHOLAS. Oh, Newman, Newman, thank you. But you're right, at least.... I must find something. Something to keep myself in shoe-leather. Before I see them. (*Cheerfully.*) Well, tomorrow, I will set about it. (*Depressed again.*) We haven't even got a place to stay.

NOGGS. Well, tonight you stay with me. Tomorrow, there's a room downstairs to let. It's hardly less a mean one than my own, but ....

NICHOLAS. Mr. Noggs. Your kindness. Unsurpassable. (*Pause.*) I have three friends. Three friends, in all the world. That bluff young fellow up in Yorkshire; Smike, yourself; and Mr. Noggs, our benefactor. (*Slight pause.*) And it is enough. It is enough, indeed. (*Nicholas drinks his drink. Smike, in imitation*

drinks his. After a second, the effect hits Smike. His eyes pop.
He bangs his chest. Nicholas and Noggs look alarmed. Firmly,
Smike puts his glass out to Mr. Noggs for more.)

Scene Four

Westminster. At once, sounds of many busy people. Set
up, on one side of the stage, the office of Sir Matthew
Pupker, consisting of a desk, an impressive map of the
world, and Sir Matthew himself, sitting on a chair, his
feet up on desk, his head covered by The Times, asleep.
This happens during the following: a sturdy Deputation,
consisting of many firm-faced Gentlemen, enters, as
Nicholas appears and speaks out front:

NICHOLAS. And the next morning, Nicholas proceeded to
the General Employment Office, in search of a position; where,
much to his surprise, he was informed that the great member of
Parliament, the renowned Sir Matthew Pupker, was seeking a
young man of conscientiousness and character, to fill the position
of his secretary, at the Palace of Westminster. (*He turns to the*
passing Deputation.) Excuse me...I have business with Sir
Matthew Pupker—
A DELEGATE. What, you as well? Come, follow me. (*The*
Deputation is at Sir Matthew's door. It knocks.)
SIR MATTHEW. Wait! (*Sir Matthew removes the Times from*
his face, adjusts the map, as Nicholas catches up with the rest of
the Deputation.) Come! (*The Deputation, and Nicholas, enter*
the room.) Gentlemen, I am rejoiced to see you. Please, come in.
(*Sir Matthew returns to his desk as the leader of the Deputation,*
a Mr. Pugstyles, pushes himself to the front.) Now, gentlemen.
I see by the newspapers that you are dissatisfied with my conduct as your member.
PUGSTYLES. Yes, we are.
SIR MATTHEW. Well, now, do my eyes deceive me? Or is that
my old friend, Pugstyles?

95

PUGSTYLES. I am that man.

SIR MATTHEW. Give me your hand, my worthy friend. Pugstyles, I am so sorry you are here.

PUGSTYLES. I am sorry too, but your conduct has rendered this deputation quite imperative.

SIR MATTHEW. My conduct, Pugstyles? You speak of my conduct?

PUGSTYLES. Yes.

SIR MATTHEW. Well, then... (*Rhetorically.*) My conduct, gentlemen, has been, and ever will be, regulated by a sincere regard for the true interests of this great and happy country. Whenever I behold the peaceful, industrious communities of our island home, I clasp my hands, and turning my eyes to the broad expanse above my head, exclaim, 'Thank heaven, that I am a Briton!' (*Long pause*).

A DELEGATE. Gammon.

SIR MATTHEW. The meaning of that term, I must confess, is quite unknown to me. But if it means you think I'm too benign, too sanguine, too complacent, sir, you would be right. (*He goes to the map and gestures.*) For e'en as we sit here, and lightly chatter, Russia's surly armies, fixed on vile conquest, surge across her borders, threatening the very jugular... Sir, do you know Kabul?

THIRD DELEGATE. No, sir.

SIR MATTHEW. Or have you met the Amir of the Afghans, he whose name is perfidy?

THIRD DELEGATE. I have not, sir.

SIR MATTHEW. Or heard the hideous war-cry of the Slavic hordes, intent on rape and pillage?

THIRD DELEGATE. No, I have not heard the Slavic hordes, sir, or their hideous war-cry.

SIR MATTHEW. Well... well then. What is the little matter you would speak of? Fishing rights, or water-rates, or timber duty? (*Pugstyles puts on his spectacles and takes out a list of questions. The rest of the Deputation also take out lists of questions, to check Pugstyles' reading.*)

PUGSTYLES. Question number one. Whether, sir, you did not give a voluntary pledge, that in the event of your being returned you would immediately put down the practice of coughing and groaning in the House of Commons. And whether you did not submit to being coughed and groaned down in the very first debate of the session? (*Pause.*)

SIR MATTHEW. Go on to the next one, my dear Pugstyles.

PUGSTYLES. Have you any explanation to offer with reference to that question, sir?

SIR MATTHEW. Certainly not. (*The Deputation looks at each other. Pugstyles breathes deeply, and continues.*)

PUGSTYLES. Question number two. Whether, sir, you did not likewise give a voluntary pledge that you would support your colleagues on every occasion; and whether you did not, the night before last, desert them and vote upon the other side, because the wife of a leader on that other side had invited Lady Pupker to an evening party? (*Pause.*)

SIR MATTHEW. Go on.

PUGSTYLES. Nothing to say on that either, sir?

SIR MATTHEW. Nothing whatever. (*Pause.*)

PUGSTYLES. So, Question number three. If, sir, you did not state upon the hustings, that it was your firm and determined intention, if elected, to vote at once for universal suffrage and triennial parliaments?

SIR MATTHEW. Oh, no!

THE DEPUTATION. Oh! Oh!

SIR MATTHEW. No, not at all. What happened was, that an illiterate voter in the crowd inquired if I would vote for universal suffering and triangular parliaments. To which I replied, in jest of course, "why, certainly." (*A groan from the Deputation.*) So, is that all?

PUGSTYLES. No. Question four. Will you resign?

SIR MATTHEW. No.

PUGSTYLES. Sorry?

SIR MATTHEW. I said, no.

PUGSTYLES. You won't resign, under any circumstances?

SIR MATTHEW. Absolutely not.

PUGSTYLES. Then . . . Then, good morning, sir. (*The Deputation turns to go.*)

SIR MATTHEW. Good morning to you all. (*As the Deputa-*

97

tion leaves.) God bless you! Every one! (*Left alone, as he thinks, Sir Matthew notices Nicholas.*) What? Who's this?

NICHOLAS. It's me, sir.

SIR MATTHEW. Ha! A secret voter! Out, sir, out, you've heard my answer. Follow out your deputation.

NICHOLAS. I should have done so if I had belonged to it.

SIR MATTHEW. (*Tossing down the map.*) You don't? Then what the devil are you in here for?

NICHOLAS. I wish to offer myself as your secretary.

SIR MATTHEW. That's all you came for, is it?

NICHOLAS. Yes.

SIR MATTHEW. You've no connection with the papers?

NICHOLAS. No.

SIR MATTHEW. And what's your name?

NICHOLAS. My name is Nickleby. (*Slight pause. Sir Matthew eyes Nicholas beadily.*)

SIR MATTHEW. Related to Ralph Nickleby?

NICHOLAS. I am.

SIR MATTHEW. Well, then, sit down.

SIR MATTHEW. So, you want to be my secretary, do you?

NICHOLAS. Yes.

SIR MATTHEW. Well, what can you do?

NICHOLAS. Well, I suppose that I can do what usually falls to the lot of other secretaries.

SIR MATTHEW. What's that?

NICHOLAS. Well, I presume, correspondence . . .

SIR MATTHEW. Good.

NICHOLAS. The arrangement of papers and documents—

SIR MATTHEW. Very good, what else?

NICHOLAS. Well, um—the general one, of making myself as agreeable and useful as I can.

SIR MATTHEW. Well, now, that's all very well, young Mr. Nickleby, as far as it goes, but it don't go far enough. I should require, for example, to be crammed, sir.

NICHOLAS. Crammed?

SIR MATTHEW. Yes, crammed. My secretary would need to make himself acquainted with all domestic and all international affairs, to scan the newspapers for paragraphs of lasting or of passing interest, for revolutions, wars, disturbances in Birmingham, "the mysterious disappearance of a potboy," on which I might found a speech or question; he would be required, as well, to study all the printed tables, and to work up arguments about the dire consequences of a raise in tax, or else the terrible result of lowering it, on why we need to increase government expenditure, on the national defence, or else decrease it, to encourage thrift among the lower classes; of gold bullion, and the supply of money, all those things it's only necessary to talk fluently about, as no-one understands 'em; and that's just a hasty, basic outline of your duties, except of course for waiting in the lobby every night, and sitting in the gallery, and pointing me out to the populace, and noting that that sleeping gentleman's none other than the celebrated and renowned Sir Matthew Pupker, and for salary, I'll say at once, although it's much more than I'm used to give, it's fifteen shillings every week and find yourself. So. Any questions? (*Pause.*)

NICHOLAS. One. While I'm performing all your duties, sir, may I inquire what you'll be doing?

SIR MATTHEW. Eh?

NICHOLAS. I said, while I'm performing all your duties, sir, may I inquire what you'll be doing? (*Pause.*)

SIR MATTHEW. Out! Get out! Out, now!

NICHOLAS. (*Turns to go.*) I'm sorry to have troubled you.

SIR MATTHEW. Well, so am I. Out, upstart! Troublemaker! (*Nicholas has been going, but he turns back.*)

NICHOLAS. Humbug.

SIR MATTHEW. Chartist!

NICHOLAS. Charlatan!

SIR MATTHEW. Potboy!

NICHOLAS. Politician! (*This is too much. Sir Matthew goes, and Nicholas does too.*)

Scene Five

The Mantalinis' workroom and showroom. In the workroom, the Milliners, Miss Knag entering, and Kate. In the

99

showroom, an Old Lord, his Young Fiance and Madame Mantalini.

MISS KNAG. Well, bless you, dear, how very clumsy you were yesterday, again.

KATE. I know, Miss Knag.

MISS KNAG. But don't you worry, I can do all that needs doing, and all you have to do is stay quiet before company and your awkwardness will not be noticed.

KATE. No, indeed.

MISS KNAG. Oh, I do take the liveliest of interests in you, dear, upon my word. It's a sister's interest, actually. It's the most singular circumstance I ever knew. (*Madame Mantalini pulls a bell pull. A bell rings.*) Ah, that's the showroom. Now, perhaps it's best dear, after yesterday, if you do not come up. (*Unlikely.*) Unless, of course, you're called for. (*Miss Knag to the showroom.*)

1st MILLINER. Well.

2nd MILLINER. *Well.*

3rd MILLINER. Has herself took a shine to you. (*The focus shifts to the showroom, as the Milliners narrate.*)

MILLINERS.

And it so happened that an old lord of great family,

Who was going to marry a young lady of no family in particular,

Came with the young lady to witness the ceremony of trying on two nuptial bonnets,

Which were presented to her by Miss Knag,

In a charming if not breathless state of palpitation.

(*Miss Knag now in the showroom. The Old Lord is very upper class, very lecherous, and a bit gaga. The Young Fiancee is not very upper class at all.*)

YOUNG FINANCEE. Well, now. How d'I look?

MADAME MANTALINI. Oh, mademoiselle, tres elegante.

MISS KNAG. Mais oui. C'est entierement exquise, n'est ce pas?

YOUNG FIANCEE. Exsqueeze?

MISS KNAG. Exquisite.

YOUNG FIANCEE Oh, yes? Is that so? (*A slight hiatus.*)

MADAME MANTALINI. So what do you think, my lord?

YOUNG FIANCEE. Yur, do you think that I'll look fitting, darling?

OLD LORD. Fitting?

YOUNG FIANCEE. For our wedding day.

OLD LORD. Oh, yes. Oh, very fitting. For our wedding day. (*The Young Fiancee blushes, grins, and pokes the Old Lord.*)

YOUNG FIANCEE. Oh, you are, really.

OLD LORD. Am I? Am I, really?

YOUNG FIANCEE. Yur, you are. (*Miss Knag a clucking, disapproving look at Madame Mantalini. The Young Fiancee notices it.*) Mm? Can I help you?

MISS KNAG. Peut-etre—

YOUNG FIANCEE. Pardon?

MISS KNAG. Would madam care to try—?

YOUNG FIANCEE. Yur, why not. (*The Young Fiancee, trying on another bonnet.*) Oh, by the way, dear Madame Mantalini?

MADAME MANTALINI. Mademoiselle?

YOUNG FIANCEE. Tell me, where is that pretty creature we saw yesterday? The young one.

MADAME MANTALINI. Pretty . . . young . . .

MISS KNAG. (*Helpfully.*) Miss Nickleby.

YOUNG FIANCEE. That's right. 'Cos if there's one thing that I can't abide, it's being waited on by frights.

MISS KNAG. Frights, no.

MADAME MANTALINI. By—what? (*Miss Knag has got there.*)

YOUNG FIANCEE. By frights. By old frights, in particular. Well, elderly. (*Pause.*)

MADAME MANTALINI. Mais oui. Certainement. Miss Knag, send up Miss Nickleby.

MISS KNAG. Bring up?

MADAME MANTALINI. Send up. You need not return.

(*Pause. Miss Knag goes out as the Young Fiancee looks at her new bonnet in the mirror.*)

YOUNG FIANCEE. Oh, yur. Mais oui. C'est entirement exquise. (*Focus shifts back to the workroom as Miss Knag enters.*)

MISS KNAG. (*To Kate.*) You're wanted in the showroom.

KATE. Me?

MISS KNAG. Yes, you. You have been Asked For.

KATE. Oh, I...very well. (*She goes to the door. Miss Knag rather obviously not following.*) Are you not coming?

MISS KNAG. I? Why should I come? A fright like me? (*Pause.*)

1st MILLINER. What's that?

2nd MILLINER. A fright?

MISS KNAG. Why should I come? You chit, you child, you upstart!

KATE. Please, Miss Knag, what have I done?

MISS KNAG. What have you done? She asks me, what she's done?

3rd MILLINER. (*Whispers to 2nd Milliner.*) What has she done?

MISS KNAG. I'll tell you what I've done, my dear Miss Nickleby, what I've done is to be, for fifteen years, the ornament of this room and the one upstairs. And what have you done? Nothing.

KATE. Well, I would not—

MISS KNAG. And never, fifteen years, have I been victim of the vile arts, a creature who disgraces us with her proceedings, and makes proper people blush to see her machinations.

KATE. Miss Knag, what have I—

MISS KNAG. Yes, here she is, look carefully...the one who everyone is talking of, the belle, the beauty...Oh, you boldfaced thing!

KATE. Miss Knag, please tell me—

MISS KNAG. I will tell you. Go! You're asked for in the showroom. Go! (*Kate stands a moment, shrugs desperately and goes out. Pause. Miss Knag throws herself into a chair. She is surrounded by Milliners.*) Oh, have I worked here, fifteen years. And to be called a fright. (*Pause.*)

102

1st MILLINER. Oh, no.
3rd MILLINER. Oh, absolutely not.
MISS KNAG. And have I laboured, all these years, to be called elderly.
2nd MILLINER. What, elderly?
1st MILLINER. Well, what a thing to say.
MISS KNAG. (*Stands.*) I hate her. I detest and hate her. Never let her speak to me again. And never let anyone who is a friend of mine have words with her. The slut. The hussy. Impudent and artful, hussy!

Scene Six

Downstage, Noggs' garret, represented by his chair. Noggs and Smike. Upstage, the Kenwigs' room, with Mrs. Kenwigs, Morleena, the two Little Kenwigses, Mr. Lillyvick and Miss Petowker. We will discover that Mr. Lillyvick has a glass of brandy and a jug of water. Enter Nicholas.

NICHOLAS. And so, with a sad and pensive air, Nicholas retraced his steps homewards.
NOGGS. Come back?
NICHOLAS. Yes, and tired to death, and might have stayed at home for all the good I've done.
NOGGS. Couldn't expect too much, one morning.
NICHOLAS. Well, I did. And so am disappointed. I see little to choose between assisting a brutal pedagogue and being a toad-eater to a mean and ignorant upstart, member or no member. Oh, Newman, show me in all this wide waste of London, any honest means by which I could at least defray the hire of our poor room; I would not shrink from it, I will do anything, except that which offends my common pride.
NOGGS. Well, then . . . I hardly know . . .
NICHOLAS. Yes? What?
NOGGS. There is a prospect I could offer. . . .
NICHOLAS. Please, dear Newman, tell me.

NOGGS. It concerns the Kenwigses, downstairs. I told them you were Mr. Johnson, thinking perhaps, your circumstances being, as it were . . .

NICHOLAS. Yes, yes.

NOGGS. And said you were a teacher, and she said, well, having talked to Mr. Kenwigs, as is only right, she said that she had long been searching for a tutor for her little ones, to teach them French as spoken by the natives, at the weekly stipend of four shillings current coin, being at the rate of a one a week per each Miss Kenwigs, with a shilling over for the baby. That's all, and I know it's beneath you, but—

NICHOLAS. Dear Newman. I accept at once. Please tell the worthy mother, now, without delay.

NOGGS. (*Delighted.*) Right, then.

(*Narration into the Kenwigs' room, in which will be Mr. Lilly-vick, Miss Petowker, Mrs. Kenwigs, Morleena, the Little Ken-wigses and Nicholas. Noggs and Smike will have gone.*)

NOGGS. And Newman hastened with joyful steps to inform Mrs. Kenwigs of his friend's acquiescence,

NICHOLAS. And soon returning, brought back word that they would be happy to see Mr. Johnson in the first floor as soon as convenient,

NOGGS. And that Mrs. Kenwigs had upon the instant sent out to secure a second-hand French grammar and dialogues,

MISS PETOWKER. Which had long been fluttering in the six-penny box at the bookstall round the corner,

MRS. KENWIGS. And that the family,

LILLYVICK. Highly excited at the prospect of this addition to their gentility,

MRS. KENWIGS. Wished the initiatory lesson to come off

MORLEENA. Immediately!

MRS. KENWIGS. Now, uncle, this is Mr. Johnson.

LILLYVICK. How d'ye do, sir?

NICHOLAS. Splendid, thank you sir.

MRS. KENWIGS. Mr. Johnson, this is Mr. Lillyvick, my uncle, The Collector Of The Water Rate.

NICHOLAS. (*Uncertain of how he is supposed to react to this intelligence.*) The Water Rate? Indeed.

104

MRS. KENWIGS. And this is Miss Petowker, of the Theatre Royal Drury Lane.

NICHOLAS. Oh, I am highly honoured. (*Wrong.*) To make, both of your aquaintances.

MRS. KENWIGS. Now, Mr. Johnson is engaged as a private master to the children, uncle.

LILLYVICK. Yes, Susan, so you said.

MRS. KENWIGS. But I hope, Mr. Johnson, that they don't boast about it to the other children, and that if they must say anything about it, they don't say no more than: "We've got a private master come to teach us at home, but we ain't proud, because ma says it's sinful." Do you hear, Morleena?

MORLEENA. Yes, ma.

MRS. KENWIGS. Then mind you recollect, and do as I tell you. Shall Mr. Johnson begin, then, uncle?

LILLYVICK. In a moment, Susan, in a moment. First, I'd like to ask a question. Sir, how do you think of French?

NICHOLAS. What do you mean, sir?

LILLYVICK. Do you view it as a good language, sir? A pretty language? Sensible?

NICHOLAS. A pretty language, certainly. And as it has a name for everything, and admits of elegant conversation on all topics, I assume it's sensible as well.

LILLYVICK. I see. (*Gesturing with his glass.*) So, what's the French for this, then, sir?

NICHOLAS. For brandy?

LILLYVICK. No, for water. As in, "water rate."

NICHOLAS. Oh, water, sir, is "l'eau."

LILLYVICK. I thought as much. You hear that, Miss Petowker? Water. Low. I don't think anything of that. I don't think anything of French at all.

MRS. KENWIGS. But, still, the children may—

LILLYVICK. Oh, yes. Oh, let them learn it. I have no wish to prevent them. (*Pause. Miss Petowker a slight smile. Mrs. Kenwigs nervously.*)

MRS. KENWIGS. Well, then ... Mr. Johnson?

NICHOLAS. Well, then ... Lesson One. (*Enter Noggs, breathless.*)

NOGGS. Oh—oh, Mr. Johnson, this is terrible—

LILLYVICK. What's this?

MRS. KENWIGS. Why, Mr. Noggs!

NOGGS. He's back again—he's gone off to your mother's—

NICHOLAS. What?

NOGGS. —your uncle, and I got the wrong day and I'm terribly—

LILLYVICK. (*To Miss Petowker.*) It's him again.

NICHOLAS. Oh, I must go there now.

NOGGS. Yes. Yes, I s'pose you must.

MRS. KENWIGS. But Mr. Johnson—

NICHOLAS. Oh—uh—mes enfants . . . on doit continuer la lecon demain. Pardon. (*To Lillyvick, taking his drink and giving it to Noggs.*) Pardon. (*Nicholas rushes out.*)

Scene Seven

The Nicklebys' house in Thames St. All that is needed is one chair for Mrs. Nickleby. Miss La Creevy, Kate and Ralph are also there. Ralph is folding up Fanny Squeers' letter.

KATE. No, I won't believe it. Never. It's a lie, that they've invented.

RALPH. No, my dear, you wrong the worthy man. These aren't inventions. Mr. Squeers has been assaulted, Nicholas is gone, the boy goes with him. It's all true.

KATE. It can't be true. Mama, how can you stand there, listening to this?

RALPH. She's no choice, my dear. Her son's committed conduct for which he might well hold up his head at the Old Bailey. (*Pause.*) And it would be my duty, if he came my way, to give him up to justice. As a man of honour and of business, I would have no other course. Though I would wish to spare the feelings of his mother, and his sister.

MISS LA CREEVY. Perhaps I'd better . . .

KATE. No, please, Miss La Creevy, stay.

RALPH. (*Suddenly, forcefully, waving the letter.*) Madam, everything combines to prove the truth of this. He steals away at night, he skulks off with an outlaw boy? Assault, and riot? Is this innocent? (*Unnoticed by anyone, Nicholas stands there.*)

MRS. NICKLEBY. Well, I don't know, I'm sure.

KATE. Oh, mother!

MRS. NICKLEBY. And I never would have thought it of him, certainly.

KATE. You never *would have* thought?

MRS. NICKLEBY. Your uncle—is your uncle, dear.

NICHOLAS. But what he says is still untrue.

RALPH. Oh. You.

MRS. NICKLEBY. Oh, Nicholas! (*Nicholas marching towards Ralph, Kate getting in the way.*)

KATE. Oh, Nicholas, be calm, consider.

NICHOLAS. What?

KATE. Please, please, consider ... and refute these accusations.

NICHOLAS. What are they? Tell me what he's said to you.

RALPH. I've said, sir, what is true. That you attacked your master, and you nearly killed him, and you ran away. (*Pause. Nicholas is calmer now.*)

NICHOLAS. I see. (*Nicholas speaks to Kate and Mrs. Nickleby, not to Ralph.*) I interfered to save a miserable creature from the vilest cruelty. In doing so, I did inflict punishment upon the wretch who was abusing him. And if the same scene was repeated now, I'd take exactly the same part. Except, that I would strike him heavier and harder.

RALPH. Hm. The penitent.

KATE. Please, Nicholas, where is this boy?

NICHOLAS. He's with me now.

RALPH. Will you restore him?

NICHOLAS. No. Not to that man. Not ever.

MRS. NICKLEBY. Oh, I don't know what to think ...

RALPH. Now, sir, you'll listen to a word or two?

NICHOLAS. Say what you like. I shan't take heed of it.

RALPH. Then I won't speak to you, but to your mother. She may find it worth her while to listen, because what I have to say is, that he, Nicholas, shall not have access to one penny of my money, or one crust of my bread, or one grasp of my hand that might save him from the gallows. I will not meet him, and I will not hear his name. I will not help him, nor help anyone who helps him. So now he knows what he has brought on you, by coming back, and as I will not ask you to renounce him, I must renounce you. (*Pause.*)

MRS. NICKLEBY. Oh, I can't help it—

RALPH. What?

MRS. NICKLEBY. I know you have been good to us. But still, I—even if he has done everything you say—

KATE. You heard what he said, mother—

MRS. NICKLEBY. Still. I can't renounce my son. I really can't. (*Pause. Mrs. Nickleby weeping.*) And all that, thinking that he'd be headmaster. . . .

RALPH. Then I'll go.

NICHOLAS. You needn't.

RALPH. Needn't I?

NICHOLAS. Because I will. (*Kate runs to Nicholas and embraces him.*)

KATE. Nicholas, oh Nicholas, don't say so, or you'll break my heart... Mama, please speak to him. Mama, don't let him go. Don't leave us here, with no-one to protect us. Please.

NICHOLAS. I can't protect you. How can I protect you?

RALPH. My dear, there is your answer.

MRS. NICKLEBY. Oh, Kate. We'll go to rack and ruin. To the workhouse, or the Refuge for the Destitute. Or Magdalen Hospital. One or the other. Or the third. (*Nicholas takes Kate's arms from him.*)

NICHOLAS. No, mother. I'm the one that's going.

KATE. (*Horrified.*) Where? Where, Nicholas?

NICHOLAS. Don't know. (*Pause.*) It is hard. To have done nothing, but to be proscribed, just like a criminal. And to be forced to leave the ones I love. It is quite hard to bear. But still, I must, or else... you're destitute.

KATE. It might be—years.

NICHOLAS. Don't know. (*Nicholas turns to go. Kate runs after him, embraces him.*)

108

KATE. Please, you won't—
NICHOLAS. I must—
KATE. You won't forget us. Everything we had. The days, the years we spent together.
NICHOLAS. (*Taking her arms from him.*) And I don't need to entreat your sympathy. I know you won't forget them.
MISS LA CREEVY. No.
NICHOLAS. (*To Ralph.*) This isn't over. You will hear from me. (*To Kate.*) Oh, my darling girl. (*Nicholas goes out, leaving Mrs. Nickleby, Miss La Creevy, and Kate.*)

Scene Eight

The street. Early morning. Bare stage. Nicholas, Smike and Noggs appear during the narration, which is delivered by members of the company who stand round, watching the scene. Nicholas and Smike have bundles. Noggs has a can.

NARRATORS.
It was a cold, foggy morning in early Spring . . .

And a few meagre shadows flitted to and fro in the misty streets.

At intervals were heard the tread of slipshod feet,

And the chilly cry of the sweep as he crept shivering to his early toil;

The sluggish darkness thickened as the day came on,

And those who had the courage to rise and peep at the gloomy street from their curtained windows,

Crept back to bed again,

And coiled themselves up to sleep.

NICHOLAS. But Nicholas and Smike were up,

NOGGS. And Newman too, who had expended a day's income on a can of rum and milk to prepare them for their journey. (*Smike shoulders the bundles.*) Which way are you going?

NICHOLAS. Kingston first.

NOGGS. And afterwards? (*Slight pause.*) Why won't you tell me?

NICHOLAS. Because I scarcely know myself.

NOGGS. I am afraid you have some deep scheme in your head.

NICHOLAS. So deep that even I can't fathom it. Don't worry, I'll write soon.

NOGGS. You won't forget?

NICHOLAS. Oh, I'm not likely to. I've not so many friends that I can grow confused about the number, and forget the very best.

NOGGS. And, despite Newman's insistence that he be allowed to walk an hour or two with them,

NICHOLAS. Nicholas and Smike eventually made their farewells and turned, and left, and turned again,

NOGGS. To see their friend still waving to them,

NICHOLAS. Till they turned the corner, and could see old Newman Noggs no more. (*Noggs has gone. Smike and Nicholas trudging on.*)

NICHOLAS. Now, listen to me, Smike. We're bound for Portsmouth.

SMIKE. Ports—mouth.

NICHOLAS. Yes, because it is a seaport town, and I am thinking we might board some ship. I'm young and active, so are you.

SMIKE. And I am very willing.

NICHOLAS. Yes, you are. Too willing, for example, with that bundle. Let me carry it a while.

SMIKE. (*Stops.*) No. No.

NICHOLAS. (*Stops.*) Why not?

SMIKE. Because I thought of carrying it. For you. (*They walk on. Narration:*)

NARRATORS.

It was by this time within an hour of noon, and although dense vapour still enclosed the city they had left,

As if to clothe its schemes of gain and profit,

In the open country it was clear and fair.

SMIKE. Hey. I—
NICHOLAS. Yes, Smike?
SMIKE. The ship. On ship. I, when I was at—that place—(*He doesn't want to name Dotheboys Hall.*)
NICHOLAS. Yes?
SMIKE. I used to milk the cows and groom the horses.
NICHOLAS. Um—it is a ship, Smike. Not that many cows and horses on board ship. Well, I don't believe... (*Smike looks at Nicholas. He gets the joke. It's infectious. Nicholas laughs too. Music plays and the Narrators sing. As they sing, Smike jumps on Nicholas' back, and the two of them career round the stage, blissfully happy.*)
NARRATORS. (*Sing.*)*

> A broad fine honest sun
> Lighted up the green pasture
> And dimpled water with the semblance of summer,
> Leaving the travellers with the freshness of spring.

> The ground seemed to quicken their feet,
> The sheep bells were music to their ears,
> And hoping made them strong
> And strength awakened hope
> And they pushed onward with the courage of lions.

> And so the day wore on
> And so the day wore on
> And so the day wore on.

(*Nicholas and Smike stop, put down the bundles, and sit.*)
NICHOLAS. Smike. Do you have a good memory?
SMIKE. I don't know. I had once, I think. But now all gone.
NICHOLAS. Why do you think you had one once?
SMIKE. Because I could remember, when I was a child.
NICHOLAS. Do you remember, when you went to Yorkshire? What the day was like. The weather, hot or cold?

* See special note on copyright page.

111

SMIKE. Wet. Very wet. And afterwards. When it was raining. I could see myself. The day I came.

NICHOLAS. Did you come there alone?

SMIKE. No. No. A man—a dark and withered man, they used to say. And I think I remember, too. Remember—being frightened of him. Glad he went away. But frightened at the place he left me, too.

NICHOLAS. Now look at me. Don't turn away. Do you remember, anything or anyone or anywhere, before that house in Yorkshire? Think, Smike, think. (*Pause.*)

SMIKE. A room. (*Slight pause.*) I slept once in a room, a large and lonesome room, beneath the attic, there was a hook in the ceiling above me. I was frightened of it, covered up my head. (*Pause.*) Used to dream. Dream terribly about the room. And people in it. Things, that changed. But that room—never changes. (*Pause.*) Till now, I have not known two days together, when I haven't been afraid. (*A Narrator—the actor who will play the Landlord, enters, as a table and a bench are brought in behind him.*)

LANDLORD. And the sun went down, and in the morning it rose up again, and they rose with it, and walked onwards, until Smike could go no further. And they found a little inn, yet twelve miles short of Portsmouth.

Scene Nine

The courtyard of a roadside inn. The Landlord, sitting on the bench beside the table. Nicholas and Smike standing there, looking bedraggled and tired.

NICHOLAS. Ah. How far to Portsmouth, sir?

LANDLORD. Twelve miles. Long miles.

NICHOLAS. A good road?

LANDLORD. No. A bad one.

NICHOLAS. We must get to Portsmouth by tonight.

LANDLORD. Well, don't let me influence you, in any way...

112

But if I were you, I wouldn't go.

NICHOLAS. You wouldn't?

LANDLORD. No.

NICHOLAS. Look, I...Look here, it's obvious enough. We are both, very humble, and we can't afford to stay the night. But if you had a little food ...?

LANDLORD. What would you like?

NICHOLAS. Cold meat?

LANDLORD. No, sorry.

NICHOLAS. Mutton chops?

LANDLORD. Clean out.

NICHOLAS. An egg?

LANDLORD. No, yesterday, had more than we could cope with. And tomorrow, mountains of 'em coming in.

NICHOLAS. Today?

LANDLORD. No eggs today. (*Enter Mr. Vincent Crummles and his sons, Master Crummles and Master P. Crummles. Mr. Crummles is a theatrical manager. His sons are dressed in sailor suits, and are presently practising a stage fight with wooden swords. The fight finishes spectacularly, with the defeat of the taller Master Crummles by the shorter Master P. Crummles. Crummles himself applauds.*)

CRUMMLES. That's capital! You'll get a double encore if you take care, boys. You'd better go and get your travelling clothes on now. (*The boys go out, one of them leaving his sword where it fell. Nicholas to the Landlord.*)

NICHOLAS. Well, then, we'll have to walk on hungry. Portsmouth, twelve bad miles. (*Nicholas and Smike turn to go.*)

CRUMMLES. Portsmouth?

NICHOLAS. Sir?

CRUMMLES. You're set for Portsmouth?

NICHOLAS. Yes, we—

CRUMMLES. So am I.

NICHOLAS. I'm pleased to hear it, sir. (*Crummles comes over.*)

CRUMMLES. And may I venture, short of money for the stage?

NICHOLAS. You've guessed it, sir.

CRUMMLES. Why, then, you'll ride with me, upon my phaeton.

NICHOLAS. Um—

CRUMMLES. That's settled. Landlord, see my pony's fetched. (*The Landlord goes out. Crummles sees the dropped sword, picks it up, and waves it.*) So, what d'you think of that, sir?

NICHOLAS. What? Oh, very good indeed. Quite—capital.

CRUMMLES. You won't see such as that too often.

NICHOLAS. No. And if they'd been, perhaps, a little better matched—

CRUMMLES. What, matched? Why sir, it's the very essence of the combat that there should be a foot or two between 'em. Otherwise, how are you to get up the sympathies of the audience in a legitimate manner?

NICHOLAS. Oh, I see. They are—you are—theatricals?

CRUMMLES. Why yes, of course. And playing Portsmouth from tonight. Yes, I am Vincent Crummles, and I am in the theatrical profession, my wife is in the theatrical profession, and my children are in the theatrical profession. I had a dog that lived and died in it from a puppy, and my chaise-pony goes on in Timour the Tartar. (*The Master Crummleses re-enter with baggage. Re-enter, too, the Landlord, and a stable-boy. During the following, they move the table, place the bench in front of it, and pile baggage on the table, so that the table is converted into the small carriage that Crummles calls his "phaeton." The final additions are two washing tubs and a water-pump, piled on top, and two reins, running out from the front of the table, which, when Crummles picks them up, will suggest the presence of the imaginary pony in front of the carriage.*) Ah, now it's just my baggage, and we're set to go.

NICHOLAS. This is—this is most generous.

CRUMMLES. Oh, not at all. It's my self-interest. I have an eye for talent, Mr. . . . .

NICHOLAS. Oh, uh, Johnson.

CRUMMLES. Johnson? And yours struck me immediately.

NICHOLAS. Talent for what?

CRUMMLES. Why, for the stage! There's genteel comedy, your walk and manner, juvenile tragedy, your eye, and touch-and-go farce in your laugh.

NICHOLAS. But, sir—

CRUMMLES. (*Dropping his voice.*) And as for your, associate,

114

I've never seen a better for the starving business. Only let him be quite tolerably well-dressed for the Apothecary—Romeo and Juliet—the slightest red dab on his nose, and he'll be guaranteed three rounds the moment he pops his head round the practicable door.

NICHOLAS. The practicable—

CRUMMLES. In the front grooves, O.P. Sir, can you write?

NICHOLAS. Well, I am not illiterate.

CRUMMLES. Well, that could not be better. You will write our new piece, for a week on Monday, if you'd be so kind. Now, boys—

NICHOLAS. But, sir—I can't—I've never written anything.

CRUMMLES. What stuff! Do you speak French?

NICHOLAS. Yes, like a native. (*Crummles takes a script from a bag and tosses it to Nicholas.*)

CRUMMLES. Then turn that into English, put your name on it, and there's the play. Oh, but for one more thing... I've just bought a real pump and two fine washing tubs—I got 'em cheap—and you must work them in. You know, the bills, we'll advertise 'em: "Splendid Tubs," "A Real Pump," that kind of thing, you'll probably be writing out the bills yourself, now are we set and can we go?

NICHOLAS. Sir, I must ask one more question. (*Crummles turns back.*)

CRUMMLES. Ask away.

NICHOLAS. Will I be paid for this?

CRUMMLES. Will you be paid? Will you be paid? Dear sir, with your own salary, your friend's, and royalties, you'll make a pound a week!

NICHOLAS. A pound a week.

CRUMMLES. At least. Now come, sirs, come. (*Nicholas turns to Smike who is looking rapt.*)

NICHOLAS. Well, Smike, what times we've fallen on, who could have . . . Smike?

SMIKE. The stage! (*Everyone now on the phaeton. Music, a light change, and horse-shoe effect from off. Crummles has picked up the reins, and everyone mimes being on a moving vehicle. The Landlord and Stable-boy have gone.*)

115

CRUMMLES. (*With a nod at the pony.*) He's a good pony at bottom.

NICHOLAS. I am sure of it.

CRUMMLES. And quite one of us. His mother was on the stage, of course.

NICHOLAS. She was?

CRUMMLES. Yes, yes, ate apple-pie at a circus for upwards of fourteen years, fired pistols, went to bed in a nightcap, and in short, took the low comedy entirely. (*Crummles, confidentially, to Nicholas.*) His father was a dancer.

NICHOLAS. Oh? Distinguished?

CRUMMLES. No, not very. The fact is, that he'd been jobbed out in the days originally, and never lost his bad habits. He was cleverish in melodrama, but too broad, too broad. And when the mother died, he took the port-wine business.

NICHOLAS. Port-wine business.

CRUMMLES. Yes, you know, the drinking of the port-wine with the clown. But he was greedy, and one night he bit the bowl right off, and choked himself to death. Vulgarity—the end of him at last. (*And they have arrived. Everyone gets off the phaeton, and the boys strike the props, bench and table, as:*) Well, here we are boys, Portsmouth, for three weeks. All men have their trials, and this is ours. Come on, boys, bustle, bustle.

NICHOLAS. And Nicholas jumped out, and, giving Smike his arm, accompanied the manager up the High Street towards the theatre, feeling nervous and uncomfortable at the prospect of an introduction to a scene so new to him. (*Nicholas follows Crummles out. Smike and the Master Crummleses follow, too.*)

Scene Ten

The stage of the Portsmouth Theatre. It is bare, and looks very dusty and dour. Enter most of the Crummles Theatre Company. They are Mr. Bane, Mr. Wagstaff, Mr. Pailey, Mr. Fluggers, Mr. Hetherington, Mr. Blightey, Miss Bravassa, Miss Belvawney, Miss Gazingi, Mrs. Lenville, and,

116

at the centre of it all, Mrs. Crummles. A moment as they survey the scene. Then Mrs. Grudden, the Stage Manager, pulls a clothes rail across the stage. A certain amount of animation follows: Mr. Bane and Mr. Hetherington fetch a chair and table for Mrs. Crummles, others open luggage, practise attitudes, look round. The bustle continues throughout the scene. Enter Crummles, Nicholas, Smike and the Master Crummleses.

CRUMMLES. Well, here we are. Good afternoon to one and all. And welcome to Portsmouth! (*The Performers look back, not very enthusiastically. Mrs. Crummles calls to her husband.*)
MRS. CRUMMLES. Vincent.
CRUMMLES. (*Going to her.*) Ah—Mrs. Crummles.
MRS. CRUMMLES. Vincent. (*They embrace. Mrs. Crummles notices Nicholas and Smike.*) Who are those men, so withered and so wild in their attire? (*Crummles whispers to Mrs. Crummles.*)
SMIKE. Is this a theatre? I thought it would be a blaze of light and finery.
NICHOLAS. Why, so it is. But not by day, Smike, not by day.
CRUMMLES. Uh, Mr. Johnson. Please, meet Mrs. Crummles. (*Nicholas and Smike come over.*)
MRS. CRUMMLES. I am so glad to see you see, so glad. And overcome to welcome you, (*To Crummles.*) provisionally, (*To Nicholas.*) as a promising new member of our corps. (*She looks at Smike.*) And this—yet more? An undernourished friend. You too are welcome, sir. (*Smike is brought forward to shake the hand of Mrs. Crummles as the Infant Phenomenon dances on. She is of doubtful age, though dressed in a little girl's ballet costume. She pirouettes and falls in an attitude of terror. She is followed on by Mr. Folair, a pantomimist, not in the first flush of youth, who wears buff slippers and is brandishing a walking stick. Mrs. Grudden appears with a list and tries to attract Mr. Crummles' attention as it becomes clear that Folair and the Phenomenon are practising a dance.*)
FOLAIR. And one and two and three—
CRUMMLES. What's this?

MRS. CRUMMLES. It's the Indian Savage and the Maiden.

FOLAIR. Pose and one and two and growl and threaten—

CRUMMLES. (*Explaining to Nicholas.*) Oh, yes, the little ballet interlude. Capital, capital.

FOLAIR. And attitude...and he loves her, and she loves him, and spin... (*The Phenomenon executes a little spin, aided by Folair. A trailing hand hits Folair in the mouth.*) ...Thank you, and climax... (*A complicated and uncertain climax, culminating with Folair kneeling, and the Phenomenon standing with one foot on his knee, her hand over his face. Crummles applauds.*)

CRUMMLES. Bravo, bravo! (*Crummles takes the Phenomenon to introduce her to Nicholas. During the following, two latecomers, Miss Snevellicci and Miss Ledrook, appear. The former is the leading young actress of the company, and knows it. She whispers to Miss Bravassa, asking her about Nicholas.*) And this, sir, is Miss Ninetta Crummles, better known to half the nobility of England, as the Infant Phenomenon.

NICHOLAS. Your daughter?

CRUMMLES. Our daughter, sir, and the idol of every place we go into. The talent of this child is not to be imagined. She must be seen, sir, seen—to be even faintly appreciated. Now, kiss your mother, dear. (*The Infant Phenomenon kisses Mrs. Crummles. Something unpleasant transfers itself from daughter to mother.*)

MRS. CRUMMLES. What has the child been eating. Mrs. Grudden? Where are you? (*Mrs. Crummles drags the Phenomenon off.*)

NICHOLAS. May I ask how old she is?

CRUMMLES. You may, sir. She is ten years of age, sir.

NICHOLAS. Not more!

CRUMMLES. Not a day.

NICHOLAS. Dear me, it's quite—extraordinary! (*Folair joins the conversation. Smike has wandered off, and soon he will be collared by Mrs. Grudden, who tries costumes on him.*)

FOLAIR. Oh, great talent, there, sir. Great talent.

NICHOLAS. Well, yes, ind—

FOLAIR. Oh, yes, she shouldn't be in the provinces, she really shouldn't.

CRUMMLES. (*Suspiciously.*) What do you mean?

FOLAIR. I mean that she is too good for country boards, and that she ought to be in one of the large houses in London, or nowhere; and I tell you more, that if it wasn't for envy and jealousy in some quarters, she would be. Perhaps you'll introduce me here, Mr. Crummles.

CRUMMLES. Mr. Folair. This is Mr. Johnson, who's to write our new piece for Monday, and when he's done that he's to study Romeo—oh, don't forget the tubs and pumps, sir, by-the-by . . . (*Crummles is presenting Nicholas with bits of script from his pockets.*) and Rover, too, of course, you might as well while you're about it, and Cassio and Jeremy Diddler. You can easily knock them off; one part helps all the others so much. Here they are, cues and all.

NICHOLAS. But—

CRUMMLES. Ah, there's Miss Belvawney. (*Crummles goes off after Miss Belvawney.*)

FOLAIR. Happy to know you, sir. (*He shakes Nicholas's hand.*) Well, did you ever see such a set-out as *that*. (*He tosses his head in the general direction of the Phenomenon and pulls a face.*)

NICHOLAS. Do you mean the Infant Phenomenon?

FOLAIR. Infant humbug, sir. With half a pint of gin a morning, every day since infancy, you could look ten for life, I'd venture.

NICHOLAS. I see. You seem to take it to heart.

FOLAIR. Yes, by Jove, and well I may. Isn't it enough to make a man crusty to see that sprawler put up in the best business every night, and actually keeping money out of the house? Why, I know of fifteen and sixpence that came to Southampton to see me dance the Highland Fling, and what's the consequence? I've never been put up in it since—never once—while the Infant Phenomenon has been grinning through artificial flowers at five people and a baby on the pit, and two boys in the gallery, every night. Oh, halloa, fellow, how are you? (*For some moments, Nicholas has been aware of Mr. Lenville, the Tragedian, fencing towards him.*)

LENVILLE. Well, Tommy, do the honours, do the honours.

FOLAIR. Ah, yes. This is Mr. Johnson, joined us suddenly, this afternoon. Mr. Lenville, who does our first tragedy.

NICHOLAS. First tragedy?

FOLAIR. Oh, yes, the major tragic roles, and—

LENVILLE. What's he joined to play, then, Tommy?

NICHOLAS. Well, I've been asked to—

FOLAIR. (*Interrupts.*) Bits and pieces, bits and pieces. Cassio, and other things, and such.

LENVILLE. What other things?

FOLAIR. And writing a new piece as well.

LENVILLE. A new piece, eh? What's in it?

NICHOLAS. Well, the play is based on a fascinating French fable—

LENVILLE. I meant for me. Something, you know, in the tragic and declamatory line—(*Luckily, Mr. Lenville has said this while looking round at other activity, so Folair can whisper to Nicholas.*)

FOLAIR. But Not Too Young.

NICHOLAS. Oh, yes. Well, sir, there is a character who turns his wife and child out of doors, and in a fit of jealousy stabs his eldest son in the library.

LENVILLE. Ah yes, that's very good.

NICHOLAS. After which, he is troubled by remorse till the last act, and then he makes up his mind to destroy himself. But just as he—or, you—are raising the pistol to your head, a clock strikes ten.

LENVILLE. I see. Yes, excellent.

NICHOLAS. You pause. You recollect to have heard a clock strike ten in your infancy. The pistol falls from your hand, you burst into tears, and become a virtuous and exemplary character for ever afterwards.

LENVILLE. Capital. Yes, sir, that will definitely serve. Ha.

FOLAIR. (*Anxiously.*) Anything for me?

NICHOLAS. (*Enjoying himself.*) Well, let me see...I imagine you would play the faithful and attached servant who is turned out of doors with the wife and child—

FOLAIR. Always coupled with that infernal phenomenon! (*He strides off. Smike, who has been dressed in a vaguely renaissance costume—a long grey gown and velvet hat—rushes forward to*

Nicholas, waving in delight, and rushes back again to Mrs. Grudden. Miss Snevellicci glides over to Nicholas.)

MISS SNEVELLICCI. I beg your pardon, sir. But did you ever play at Canterbury?

NICHOLAS. Uh . . . No, never.

MISS SNEVELLICCI. It's just—I recollect meeting a gentleman at Canterbury, only for a few moments, for I was leaving the company as he joined it, so like you that I felt almost certain it was the same.

NICHOLAS. Well, I do assure you that you are mistaken, for I'm certain, if we had met, I'd remember it.

MISS SNEVELLICCI. Oh, I'm sure that's very flattering of you to say so. But now, as I look at you again, I see that gentleman had not your eyes. You'll think me foolish, doubtless, that I take notice of such things.

NICHOLAS. Why, not at all. How can I feel otherwise than flattered by your notice in any way?

MISS SNEVELLICCI. Oh, Mr. Johnson. All you men are such vain creatures, aren't you? Mm? (*Snevellicci has been gesturing with a hand to Miss Ledrook, who refuses to come over, so Snevellicci turns and calls.*) Led, my dear.

MISS LEDROOK. Yes, what is it?

MISS SNEVELLICCI. It's not the same.

MISS LEDROOK. The same what?

MISS SNEVELLICCI. He never was at Canterbury, come here, I want to speak to you. (*Crummles appears. Miss Ledrook doesn't move, so Miss Snevellicci has to go to her, and they have a little argument, as:*)

CRUMMLES. A genius, sir, a genius. I'm thinking, that we will bring out your new piece for her bespeak.

NICHOLAS. Bewhat?

CRUMMLES. Her benefit, when her friends and patrons bespeak the play. In fact, sir, you might do us some other little assistance. There is a little—what shall I call it—a little Canvassing on these occasions—

NICHOLAS. Among the friends and patrons? (*Miss Snevellicci aware of this conversation.*)

CRUMMLES. Yes, just half an hour tomorrow morning, calling

121

on the houses, drumming up support... You know, new author, all the way from London, book now to avoid a disappointment, all that kind of thing ...

NICHOLAS. Now, sir, I am afraid that I should not like to do that.

CRUMMLES. Not even with the infant?

NICHOLAS. No. (*Miss Snevellicci rushes to Crummles and Nicholas.*)

MISS SNEVELLICCI. Oh, Mr. Johnson. Sir, you surely aren't so cruel, so heartless... and after I have been so looking forward to it, too.

NICHOLAS. Well, I'm very sorry, but—(*Mrs. Crummles sails in.*)

MRS. CRUMMLES. What's this? A problem, with the canvass?

CRUMMLES. Yes, dear. Mr. Johnson seems to have objections.

MRS. CRUMMLES. What? Object? Can this be possible?

NICHOLAS. Well, it's—

MRS. CRUMMLES. This Mr. Johnson, is it, with objections? This one, plucked, as 'twere, from dank obscurity, took off the streets—the highway—and presented with a chance that half of London would donate a vital limb for? Vincent, this is inconceivable. I am convinced his sense of what is proper, nay is chivalrous, nay once again is gallant, all will sweep him to enlistment in this noble cause. (*Looking at Nicholas. Slightly coquettishly.*) Is this not so?

NICHOLAS. Well... It is not in my nature to resist any entreaty, unless it is to do something positively wrong. I know nobody here, and nobody knows me. So be it, then. I yield.

MRS. CRUMMLES. (*With a look at Crummles, as if to say, "must I cope with everything?"*) Well. There. (*And Mrs. Crummles, Crummles and Miss Snevellicci leave Nicholas, and join the company. Nicholas now sees the full Company ranged before him.*)

MRS. GRUDDEN. Quiet. Quiet, everybody!

CRUMMLES. Ladies and gentlemen! May I introduce to you Mr. Johnson and Mr.—

NICHOLAS. (*Giving a new name to Smike.*) Digby.

CRUMMLES. Thank you. Mr. Johnson, you have met Mr. Folair

and Mr. Lenville, Miss Snevellicci and my wife and family. This is Mr. Bane, who does the tenor lovers; (*Mr. Bane waves weakly.*) Mr. Wagstaff, who's our virtuous old gentleman; (*Mr. Wagstaff is holding a suitcase, and as he stands to nod at Nicholas, we hear the clink of many bottles inside it. This confirms the impression that his red nose and uncertain gait has already given us.*) And Mr. Fluggers, who does the cloth, and can do everything from country parsons to the Pope. (*Mr. Fluggers looks up from his newspaper.*) Now, that is Mr. Blightey, who's irascible—

BLIGHTEY. (*Benignly.*) Hallo.

CRUMMLES. Mr. Hetherington, who swaggers, and Mr. Pailey who is country comical; (*Mr. Pailey grins.*) There's Miss Ledrook, who's our secondary romance, Miss Belvawney, who does the pages in white hose; Mrs. Lenville, who's the wife to Mr. Lenville; Miss Bravassa, Miss Gazingi, and Mrs. Grudden. Now, tomorrow morning, ten o'clock, we'll call The Mortal Struggle and then it's all the Chorus for the Raising of the Siege of Ghent. Good evening, everyone! (*As all the Company except for the Crummles Family itself disperse:*)

MRS. GRUDDEN. Ten o'clock, call, ten o'clock, The Mortal Struggle. Half past Siege of Ghent. All those lodgings, go to 'em. All those without, see me. Good evening, everyone. (*Mrs. Crummles leads her Family to Nicholas and Smike. Nicholas a little shrug, which Mrs. Crummles interprets as a request that he should be put out of his agony.*)

MRS. CRUMMLES. Yes, sir, I think you'll do. (*Crummles relieved. The Family sweep out. Nicholas and Smike follow.*)

Scene Eleven

The Mantalinis' showroom. The mirror, a clothes rail, clothes stands, and tailors' dummies. Miss Knag crossly fiddling about. Enter Kate.

KATE. Um, Miss—

MISS KNAG. Oh, well. If it isn't that young and pretty creature, Miss Kate Nickle—

KATE. Please, Miss Knag. You're wanted in the workroom.

MISS KNAG. Workroom. Thank you. (*As she goes.*) Well, one might have thought, some people would have had the sensitivity, to seek alternative employment. Yes, one might have thought, but it's a queer world. (*Miss Knag goes out. Enter Madame Mantalini.*)

MADAME MANTALINI. (*Adjusting a dress on a stand.*) Well, Miss Nickleby, and how are you?

KATE. I'm quite well, thank you, Madame Mantalini. (*Kate starting to help.*)

MADAME MANTALINI. Hm. I wish that I could say the same.

KATE. Why, Madame Mantalini, what's the matter?

MADAME MANTALINI. Nothing, nothing. Now, get these things in order, do. (*Mantalini's head pops into the room.*)

MANTALINI. Now, is my life-and-soul here present?

MADAME MANTALINI. No.

MANTALINI. But how can that be so, when I see it blooming in the room before me like a little rose in a demd flowerpot? So, may its poppet enter?

MADAME MANTALINI. No, he may not. For he knows he's not allowed in here. So, go along. (*Mantalini enters the room and embraces Madame Mantalini.*)

MANTALINI. Oh, will it vex itself?

MADAME MANTALINI. I said that—

MANTALINI. Will it twist and crunch its little face?

MADAME MANTALINI. Oh, I can't bear you—

MANTALINI. What, can't bear me? I, whose only joy is gaining such a lovely creature, such a Venus, such a demd enchanting, and bewitching, and engrossing, capitivating little Venus?

MADAME MANTALINI. (*Breaking away.*) Mantalini, you, your debts, extravagances, they will ruin me.

MANTALINI. (*Airily.*) Oh, that. Oh, it's a nothing, money will be made, and if it don't get made, enough, old Nickleby can stump up once again, or else I'll cut his jugular from ear to—

MADAME MANTALINI. Hush. Hush, don't you see?

MANTALINI. Oh. Dear Miss Nickleby. Well, I'll be demd. (*Pause.*) Well, then, as I am commanded, and quite demnibly

124

admonished, by my little rapture...I'll withdraw. (*He goes to the door. Then turns back.*) Unless...My little joy and bliss... Would care to join her slave for breakfast? (*Pause. Then, after a look to Kate, Madame Mantalini follows Mantalini to the door. He holds it open for her to go through. Pause. Kate carries on, working alone, for a moment. Then a new head pops round the door. It belongs to Mr. Scaley, a rather rough-and-ready, though completely professional, gentleman.*)

SCALEY. Psst.

KATE. Oh! What?

SCALEY. (*Coming into the room.*) Please don't alarm yourself, Miss. Is this the millinery concern, proprietor one Mister Muntlehiney?

KATE. Yes, what do you want?

SCALEY. (*Calling out of the door.*) Yes, Mr. Tix, we have the right establishment. (*Enter Mr. Tix, another professional gentleman. Kate, fearing that these men are thieves, backing away.*) Oh, please don't go yet, Miss. I haven't yet presented you my card. (*He hands a square, white card to Kate.*) My name is Scaley. This is Mr. Tix. Perhaps you'd be so kind as to aquaint your guv'nor with our presence. (*Kate backs to the wall and pulls the bell pull. Bell rings.*) Thank you ever so. (*Pause. Kate stands there, by the bell pull. Mr Tix is looking up at the ceiling.*)

TIX. I like the ceiling. Nice high ceiling.

SCALEY. Isn't it.

TIX. A boy could grow up here, grow up to be a man, a tall 'un too, and never bump his head on that.

SCALEY. Now, that is very true. (*Tapping a mirror.*) Good plate here, Tix.

TIX. Oh, yur. (*Fingering a dress.*) And this here article weren't put together without outlay of considerable expense, nor, neither. (*Pause as they continue looking round the room. Then Tix, to lighten the atmosphere, to Kate.*) And a very pretty colour. (*Enter Madame Mantalini.*)

MADAME MANTALINI. Kate, what's the—oh? Oh!

SCALEY. Ah. Mrs. Muntlehinney?

KATE. Madame.

SCALEY. Scaley. (*He waves at Tix.*) Mr. Tix. (*He waves a*

document.) This is a writ of execution, and if it's not immediately convenient to settle, we'll set to work at once, please, taking the inventory. (*Madame Mantalini stumbles in horror, grabs the bell, pulls it, and falls into a chair. Kate to her.*) Oh, dear. I do suspect, Tix, that we'd better make a brisk commencement. (*Tix has already taken out his inventory book. He stands behind a dress on a stand, to note its features, so that, to us, he appears to be wearing it.*)

TIX. Dress. One. Fetching shade of blue. (*Enter Mantalini.*)

SCALEY. Ah. Um, monsieur? (*Mantalini stands there a moment. He is not unused to this situation, or to men like Scaley and Tix.*)

MANTALINI. So, what's the total, demn you?

TIX. Fifteen hundred, twenty-seven pound, and four and ninepence ha'penny.

MANTALINI. The ha'penny be demd.

SCALEY. By all means. And the ninepence, too. But with regard to the outstanding...? (*Mantalini shrugs, and waves his hand. Madame Mantalini is in tears.*)

SCALEY. Oh, well. I fear that Mrs. Tix and all the little Tixes'll be minus their papa a day or two.

TIX. (*Looks around.*) Or even three.

SCALEY. (*To comfort Madame Mantalini.*) Now, come on, madam, take a little consolation, for I'll warrant half of this stuff in't been paid for, eh? (*Scaley and Tix set about their business as Mantalini goes to his wife.*)

TIX. Two cheval-glasses. One with damaged frame.

MANTALINI. Now, dear, my cup of happiness's sweetener, will you listen to me for two minutes?

MADAME MANTALINI. (*Suddenly, in great passion.*) Oh, don't you speak to me. You've ruined me, and that's enough.

TIX. Three bonnets. Styling, various.

MANTALINI. (*Recoiling, as if from a blow.*) What? Do not speak to you? All this, and I, your drudge and potboy, I am not to speak to you? (*Kate looking at Mantalini with some cynicism, as are Messrs. Scaley and Tix.*)

TIX. One bust. A Roman gentleman.

MANTALINI. Oh, it's too much. Too much! (*Mantalini rushes*

from the room. Madame Mantalini stands, quickly.)

MADAME MANTALINI. Quick! Quick, Miss Nickleby! Make haste, for heaven's sake, he will destroy himself. (*She runs to the exit.*) I spoke unkindly to him, and he cannot bear it. Alfred, Alfred! (*She runs out. Suddenly, chase music. Mantalini, who has found a pair of scissors, runs on, pursued by Milliners and Madame Mantalini. The chase goes all round the stage, and even, if possible, into the auditorium, before arriving back in the showroom.*)

MANTALINI. No, I'm going to do it. Right now. No question. Going to do it. Yes, I'm going to do it. I will do it now! (*Everyone is back in the showroom. Miss Knag appears on the sidelines. Mr. Scaley and Mr. Tix carry on their work calmly.*)

1st MILLINER. Eh, what's he doing?

2nd MILLINER. Got my scissors.

1st MILLINER. Lor.

MADAME MANTALINI. (*Flinging her arms round her husband.*) Oh, Alfred, stop, I didn't mean to say it, promise you, I didn't mean to say . . .

2nd MILLINER. That's highly dangerous.

MANTALINI. I have brought ruin on the best and purest creature ever threw herself away on some demned vagabond. I'll do it! Demmit, let me go! (*He pulls himself away from her.*)

MADAME MANTALINI. Compose yourself, my angel, please, someone, disarm him! (*Mantalini raises the scissors, to plunge them in his breast. The two Milliners, without much difficulty, grab him and disarm him.*)

2nd MILLINER. Now, come on, Mr. Mantalini—

1st MILLINER. Drop the scissors, like a nice man.

2nd MILLINER. There!

MANTALINI. No! No! You, fetch me poison!

2nd MILLINER. Poison?

MADAME MANTALINI. It was no-one's fault.

MANTALINI. (*Banging his head against an absent wall.*) Fetch me a pistol. You, ma'am, blow my brains out.

1st MILLINER. Me?

MADAME MANTALINI. It was my fault as much as yours— (*Mantalini grabs the scissors back from the 2nd Milliner.*)

127

2nd MILLINER. Hey—

MANTALINI. Rope! A rope to hang myself—(*He tries to hang himself by the bell pull. The bell rings. He looks at Madame Mantalini.*) What did you say?

MADAME MANTALINI. I said—that it was no-one's fault. Or, if it was, then mine as much as yours. My love. (*Pause. Mantalini raises the hand, in which he holds the scissors.*)

MANTALINI. Oh, my little pepperpot. Demnation, gravy-boat. (*He drops the scissors.*)

SCALEY. One pair, scissors . . .

MANTALINI. My—little—apfel strudel. (*Madame Mantalini aware for the first time of the open-mouthed Milliners and the faintly smiling Miss Knag.*)

MADAME MANTALINI. Please, now, Alfred. Come. (*Madame Mantalini puts out her hand to Mantalini. He walks to her, and they go out together. Miss Knag picks up the scissors.*)

1st MILLINER. Well, hark at that.

2nd MILLINER. Well, hark at *her*.

MISS KNAG. Well, now, young ladies. After all this, wild excitement, shall we return, and recommence our labours? Hm? (*The Milliners turn out front to narrate.*)

MILLINERS.

And return they did, but after half an hour they were informed their services would be immediately dispensed with;

And on the next day Mr. Mantalini's name appeared among the list of bankrupts;

And on the third day, the young ladies were all re-engaged,

Except for Miss Kate Nickleby.

MISS KNAG. (*Maliciously, to Kate.*) Miss Nickleby. I think *you* needn't recommence your labours. I think that *you* Need Not Return. (*She goes out, the Milliners go out too, and finally Kate.*)

Scene Twelve

Portsmouth, various locations. Bare stage. Enter Nicholas.

NICHOLAS. And at the hour next morning stipulated for the canvassing of Miss Snevellicci's friends and patrons, Nicholas repaired to the lodgings of that lady, which were at the house of a tailor in Smollet St. And having been admitted to her apartments by the tailor's daughter, he was told to wait. (*Enter Miss Snevellicci, carrying a pile of sheets and towels, and, on top of them, a scrapbook. She is followed by the Infant Phenomenon.*)
MISS SNEVELLICCI. Oh, Mr. Johnson. Please forgive me. We're all at sixes and sevens this morning.
NICHOLAS. Oh, I'm sorry to—
MISS SNEVELLICCI. My darling Led—Miss Ledrook, from the company . . .
NICHOLAS. Oh, yes.
MISS SNEVELLICCI. —was taken so ill in the night, we had to all move rooms. I thought she would expire, there, in my arms!
NICHOLAS. Well, such a fate is almost to be envied. But—
MISS SNEVELLICCI. Oh, Mr. Johnson, what a flatterer you are. (*Miss Snevellicci, moving towards the exit, artfully drops the scrapbook.*) Oh, dear, look—
NICHOLAS. (*Picking up the scrapbook.*) Allow me, please.
MISS SNEVELLICCI. Oh, thank you, sir. Forgive me for a moment. (*Miss Snevellicci goes out. Nicholas reads the scrapbook.*)
NICHOLAS.
"Sing, God of Love, and tell me in what dearth,
Thrice-gifted Snevellicci came on earth,
To thrill us with her smile, her tear, her eye,
Sing, God of Love, and tell me quickly why."
(*Miss Snevellicci has reappeared, without the sheets and towels.*)
MISS SNEVELLICCI. Mr. Johnson!
NICHOLAS. Oh, I'm—
MISS SNEVELLICCI. Mr. Johnson, I'm surprised at you.

NICHOLAS. I'm sorry, I—

MISS SNEVELLICCI. You are a cruel creature, I'm ashamed to look you in the face.

NICHOLAS. I thought, perhaps... You'd dropped it here on purpose?

MISS SNEVELLICCI. Mr. Johnson. I would not have had you see it For The World. Now, shall we go? (*Nicholas out front, as Miss Snevellicci and the Phenomenon move to the area which will represent the home of the Curdles.*)

NICHOLAS. And go at once they did, and the first house to which they bent their steps was situated in a terrace of respectable appearance, where lodged the Curdles, to whose apartments they were instantly directed. (*Nicholas joins the Phenomenon and Miss Snevellicci.*)

MISS SNEVELLICCI. Now, Mrs. Curdle is well-known to have quite the London taste in matters relating to the drama; and as to Mr. Curdle, he has written a pamphlet of sixty-four pages,

NICHOLAS. (*Out front.*) Proving that by altering the received mode of punctuation, any one of Shakespeare's plays could be made quite different, and the sense completely changed. (*Enter Mr. and Mrs. Curdle. Mr. Curdle has a chair for his wife, who sits.*)

CURDLE. To be or not? To be that, is the question! Hm?

NICHOLAS. Oh, yes, indeed.

MRS. CURDLE. Dear Miss Snevellicci, and how do you do?

MISS SNEVELLICCI. Oh, I'm alarming well, dear Mrs. Curdle, and ventured to call for the purpose of asking whether you would put your name to my bespeak.

MRS. CURDLE. Oh, I really don't know what to say .... It's not as if, now is it, that the theatre was in high and palmy days—the drama's gone, perfectly gone.

MISS SNEVELLICCI. Well, p'raps, but surely—

CURDLE. As an exquisite embodiment of the poet's visions, and laying upon a new and magic world before the mental eye, the drama is gone, perfectly gone.

MRS. CURDLE. What man is there now living who can present before us all those changing and prismatic colours with which the character of Hamlet is invested?

CURDLE. What man indeed—upon the stage; why, Hamlet! Pooh! He's gone, perfectly gone. (*Pause.*)

MISS SNEVELLICCI. The play is new.

MRS. CURDLE. Oh, yes, what is the play?

MISS SNEVELLICCI. A new one, written by this gentleman, and in which he will make his first appearance on the stage.

CURDLE. I trust he has preserved the unities.

NICHOLAS. The piece is in French—originally—there is an abundance of incident, sprightly dialogue, well-fleshed, three-dimensional characters, two tubs, a pump—

CURDLE. All unavailing—pump and all—without the unities.

NICHOLAS. May I inquire, sir, as to what are the unities?

CURDLE. The unities, sir, are a completeness—a kind of universal dove-tailedness, and oneness, and general warmth, and harmony, and tone . . .

MISS SNEVELLICCI. And I am sure that Mr. Johnson will preserve the unities—all three of them—most closely. May I put your names . . . ?

CURDLE. (*Taking a sheet of paper from Miss Snevellicci.*) Well, I suppose . . . We must accept it as our duty to the drama, even if —Four Shillings?

MISS SNEVELLICCI. Yes, that's right.

MRS. CURDLE. Four shillings for *one box?*

MISS SNEVELLICCI. Yes, that's correct.

CURDLE. Four shillings for *one play?* (*Miss Snevellicci looks desperately at Nicholas.*)

NICHOLAS. Well. With a lot of people in it. (*Slight pause.*) And it is very long.

CURDLE. Well, it had better be.

NICHOLAS. (*Out front.*) And Miss Snevellicci took the money with many smiles and bends, and Mr. Curdle rang the bell as a signal for breaking up the conference. (*The Curdles going.*)

CURDLE. Oh, what? A rogue and peasant slave, am I? (*Exit the Curdles.*)

NICHOLAS. What odd people.

MISS SNEVELLICCI. Oh, I assure you, Mr. Johnson, they get even odder. (*Miss Snevellicci and the Phenomenon leaving during:*)

131

NICHOLAS. As indeed they did, and three hours later, with two pounds and nine shillings taken—

MISS SNEVELLICCI. (*Calls.*) And a further ten and sixpence definitely promised—

NICHOLAS. Nicholas repaired, as he had been instructed, to the lodgings of the Vincent Crummleses. (*Enter Crummles in a dressing gown.*)

CRUMMLES. Ah, Johnson, there you are. Come in, come in. How goes it, Johnson?

NICHOLAS. Uh—the canvass?

CRUMMLES. No, the play.

NICHOLAS. It's not quite finished yet.

CRUMMLES. Thank heavens.

NICHOLAS. Oh?

CRUMMLES. I have another novelty, that must at all costs be included, in a prominent position.

NICHOLAS. Uh . . . I'm sorry, I can't guess.

CRUMMLES. What would you say to a young lady up from London? Say, Miss Someone, of the Theatre Royal, Drury Lane?

NICHOLAS. Well, that would look excellently, on the bills.

CRUMMLES. Exactly. (*Crummles produces a poster, unrolls it, on which is prominently displayed the name of Miss Petowker, of the Theatre Royal, Drury Lane.*) So, what d'you think of that?

NICHOLAS. Dear me, Miss Petowker, I know that lady.

CRUMMLES. Then you are acquainted, sir, with as much talent as was ever compressed into one young person's body. The Blood Drinker, sir, the Blood Drinker will die with that girl; and she's the only sylph *I* ever saw who could stand upon one leg, and play the tambourine on her other knee, *like* a sylph.

NICHOLAS. When is she expected?

CRUMMLES. Why, today. She is an old friend of Mrs. Crummles's, who taught her, as it happens, everything she knows. And here she comes. (*Mrs. Crummles entering.*) You're probably aware that Mrs. Crummles was the original Blood Drinker.

NICHOLAS. I didn't know that, no.

MRS. CRUMMLES. Why, yes indeed, sir. I was obliged to give it up, however.

NICHOLAS. Oh, I'm sorry, why?

MRS. CRUMMLES. Oh, the audiences, sir. They couldn't stand it. It was too tremendous. Vincent, there's a letter here—from Miss Petowker.

CRUMMLES. Ah. (*Crummels reads the letter. Nicholas feels it necessary to converse with Mrs. Crummles.*)

NICHOLAS. You teach, I gather, ma'am.

MRS. CRUMMLES. Oh, yes, I do. In fact, I did receive some pupils here in Portsmouth, on a previous occasion. I imparted some tuition in the art of acting to the daughter of a dealer in marine provisions. Sadly, it emerged that all the time she was coming to me she'd been totally insane.

NICHOLAS. Insane! How—most extraordinary.

MRS. CRUMMLES. Well, I thought so too, until I learnt she was of the strong opinion she was living on the moon, which sad delusion went a long way to explain the style of her performances, which were distinctly lunar. So, then, Vincent. it *is* true! (*For Mr. Crummles has finished the letter.*)

CRUMMLES. Well, so it must appear. Who would have thought it?

MRS. CRUMMLES. I would, Vincent. Any woman would. It is— demonstrably—her mission.

MISS PETOWKER. (*Off.*) Mrs. Crummles! Mr. Crummles!

MRS. CRUMMLES. Ah, and here she is. Boys, boys! (*The Master Crummleses run on, and help Miss Petowker and her luggage into the room.*)

MISS PETOWKER. Oh, Mrs. Crummles, Mr. Crummles...Oh, why, Mr. Johnson!

MRS. CRUMMLES. You two are acquainted?

NICHOLAS. Yes, we ...

MISS PETOWKER. Mr. *Johnson.* We met—oh, I don't recall, on two or three occasions, Lady—Thing, and Mrs. Whatsit's salon, at the opera ... Well, Mr. Johnson, what a pleasure. (*Nicholas is embraced by Miss Petowker. Miss Petowker to Mrs. Crummles.*) Why, Mrs. Crummles, I had no *idea*. ...

MRS. CRUMMLES. We are all quite delighted, Henrietta, with The News.

MISS PETOWKER. (*Confidentially.*) Oh, but now, Mrs. Crummles, there must be now *word,* no *hint,* of anything. ...

133

MRS. CRUMMLES. My lips, my dear, are glued. Now, at this instant, dinner. (*Mrs. Crummles has been escorting Miss Petowker into another room. She changes her mind, however, and turns back to Nicholas, who is moving towards the door.*) Mr. Johnson?

NICHOLAS. Mrs. Crummles?

MRS. CRUMMLES. We have but a shoulder of mutton with onion sauce but such as our dinner is, we beg you to partake of it.

NICHOLAS. Oh, Mrs. Crummles, I should be delighted.

MRS. CRUMMLES. (*As she escorts Miss Petowker out.*) Then let the mutton and onion sauce appear! (*Exit the two women as the Master Crummles and the Phenomenon run on and drag Nicholas into dinner.*)

Scene Thirteen

Ralph Nickleby's office. To one side, Ralph's desk and chairs either side, in one of which Ralph sits, working. To the other side, a high stool and ledger table, on which are account books and a bell. This is Noggs' room, and we imagine the two rooms are divided. Noggs is in Ralph's part of the office. Mr. Mantalini is banging the bell on Noggs' desk. Noggs goes out of the "door" and round into his own area.

MANTALINI. What a demnation long time you have kept me ringing at this confounded old cracked tea-kettle of a bell, every tinkle of which is enough to throw a strong man into blue convulsions.

NOGGS. Didn't hear it more than once, myself.

MANTALINI. Then you are most demnibly and outrageously deaf. Now, where's Ralph Nickleby?

NOGGS. Might not be home. What purpose?

MANTALINI. (*Striding past Noggs to Ralph's office.*) Purpose? It's to melt some dirty scraps of paper into bright and shining, clinking, trinkling demd mint sauce. (*Ralph Nickleby looks at Mr. Mantalini.*) Ah. Nickleby. You are at home. (*Ralph a look at Noggs, who has followed.*)

NOGGS. (*Shrugs.*) He wouldn't wait. (*Ralph tosses his head at Noggs. Noggs returns to his desk.*)

MANTALINI. Well, Nickleby, you're looking well today. You look quite juvenile and jolly, demmit!

RALPH. What do you want with me?

MANTALINI. Demnation discount.

RALPH. Money's scarce.

MANTALINI. Demnd scarce, or else I wouldn't want it.

RALPH. But—as you're a friend . . . Bills of exchange?

MANTALINI. Yes, two. One for £40, and one for thirty-five.

RALPH. So, seventy-five in all. When are they due for payment?

MANTALINI. Two months one, the other four.

RALPH. Names of the guarantors? (*Mantalini hands over the bills. The front doorbell rings again. Noggs goes to answer it.*) Well, they are not cast-iron . . . But they're safe enough. I'll give you fifty for 'em.

MANTALINI. Only fifty.

RALPH. Yes.

MANTALINI. Not even, just a little more, as we are friends . . .

RALPH. But this is business, Mr. Mantalini. You'll not get a better rate. (*Noggs admits Madame Mantalini and Miss Knag.*) And so? Do you accept?

MANTALINI. I must.

RALPH. (*Opening a cash box.*) Well, then . . . (*Madame Mantalini, followed by Miss Knag, has strode in past Noggs and into Ralph's office.*)

MADAME MANTALINI. Oh, here you are.

MANTALINI. Oh. You.

MADAME MANTALINI. Yes. Me. Forgive us, Mr. Nickleby, for this intrusion. Which is attributable to the gross and most improper misbehaviour of, of Mr. Mantalini. (*Mantalini stands and tries to embrace Madame Mantalini.*)

MANTALINI. What's this you're saying, juice of pine-apple?

MADAME MANTALINI. No, none of that. I won't allow it. I will not be ruined by your profligacy any more. (*Mantalini sits.*) Mr. Nickleby, I call on you to witness what I'm going to say.

RALPH. Pray, do not ask me, madam. Settle it among yourselves.

135

MADAME MANTALINI. Well, settle it is what I plan to do. (*To Mantalini.*) This morning, you appropriated, from my desk, some bills belonging to the company, without permission. Is that not the case?

MANTALINI. It is, my precious, it is true, my tulip. I'm the demdest villain ever lived.

MADAME MANTALINI. And, knowing of my debts and obligations, caused by your extravagance, you have come here to change those bills of mine to cash. Do you deny it?

MANTALINI. No, I cannot. Oh, I'll fill my pockets up with ha'pennies, and drown myself.

MADAME MANTALINI. Well then, I tell you, Mr. Nickleby, Miss Knag, once and for all, that I never will supply this man's extravagance again. (*Pause. Mantalini looks up at his wife. He says nothing.*) I have been his dupe and his fool for long enough, and in future, he shall support himself if he can, and he may spend all that he pleases, and on whom he likes, but it shall not be mine.

MANTALINI. What are you saying, seraphim?

MADAME MANTALINI. I am insisting on a separation.

RALPH. Madam, you are not in earnest.

MADAME MANTALINI. Oh, I am.

RALPH. Madam, consider. A married woman has no property. The company belongs to Mr. Mantalini.

MADAME MANTALINI. Oh, no, sir. It does not. That company is bankrupt. But, to save what little has been left, of the furnishings and stock, I was obliged to call upon another party, who had, I'm pleased to say, sufficient capital to meet outstanding bills, to re-employ the staff, and to engage me as the manager of her new company.

MISS KNAG. New company. (*Slight pause. Mantalini looks at Miss Knag in horror.*) Yes, it's quite true, Mr. Nickleby. It's very true indeed. And I never was more glad in all my life, that I had the strength of mind to resist all offers of marriage, however advantageous, than I am when I think of my present position as compared with your most unfortunate and most undeserved one, Madame Mantalini. (*To Ralph.*) Otherwise, where would I be today?

MANTALINI. Oh, demmit, demmit, will it not slap and pinch the envious dowager, that dares so to reflect upon its own delicious?

MADAME MANTALINI. No, of course not. For Miss Knag is now, perforce, my very greatest friend.

MANTALINI. This is a dream, a demned, demned horrid dream.

MADAME MANTALINI. You have brought it on yourself.

MANTALINI. Oh, has it come to this? Oh, have I cut my heart into a demned extraordinary number of little pieces, and given them away one after another to the same little engrossing captivator, and it's come to this?

MADAME MANTALINI. It has. You know it has. (*Slight pause. Madame Mantalini goes to Ralph and puts out her hand. Ralph hands over the Bills of Exchange. Miss Knag trots over, and puts out her hand. Madame Mantalini gives the Bills to Miss Knag. To Ralph.*) I did...A long time. I did love that creature, Mr. Nickleby. (*Madame Mantalini and Miss Knag go out. Mantalini runs, and cries after them.*)

MANTALINI. Oh, I will drown myself! (*But they have gone. Back to Ralph.*) Oh, Nickleby, how can you sit there, watching such a cruel, brazen chick-a-biddy savaging the very heart of one who—

RALPH. Come, sir, you must put away these fooleries, now.

MANTALINI. You—what?

RALPH. And live by your own wits again. (*Pause.*)

MANTALINI. But, demmit, you'll help me, won't you, Nickleby?

RALPH. No, I will not. Good day.

MANTALINI. You can't be serious.

RALPH. I seldom joke. Good day.

MANTALINI. Now, look here, Nickleby, you know, without me, you'd've not got one brass farthing out of—

RALPH. Without you, sir, my credit would not have been needed. As you well know. And now, good day to you. (*Pause.*)

MANTALINI. Well. Well, demnation—cruelty. (*He makes to go, turns back. He can't believe it.*) It's over. (*Mantalini goes out.*)

RALPH. Hm. Love him. Love that. All love, is cant and vanity. (*Noggs has appeared. He coughs.*) Yes, what?

NOGGS. (*Presenting a card to Ralph.*) Two gentlemen. Are out the back. Their card. (*Enter Mr. Scaley and Mr. Tix.*)

SCALEY. Well, good day, Mr. Nickleby. Here is the tally. Thirteen hundred pounds. That's plus or minus the odd bonnet, or an underskirt or two.

RALPH. I thank you.

SCALEY. And dare I venture, you'll be kindly helping out the business once again? Another loan? And in a threemonth, when the interest falls due . . .

RALPH. No, I think not, Mr. Scaley. There has been a change of ownership. The business is now in more able hands.

TIX. Oh, dear.

SCALEY. Oh, very sorry, sir.

RALPH. So, then, your task's complete. How much? (*Scaley hands Ralph a bill, which Ralph signs and hands back to Scaley.*)

SCALEY. It's always such a pleasure doing business with you, Mr. Nickleby.

TIX. It's such a joy.

Scene Fourteen

Portsmouth. In the wings of the theatre. The Crummles Company runs on from their curtain call. We hear applause. They have been performing Nicholas' play for Miss Snevellicci's benefit. The women are mostly clustering round Nicholas, the Men round Miss Petowker. Smike looks on.

MISS GAZINGI. Oh, Mr. Johnson, what a triumph.

NICHOLAS. Well, I—Was it?

MISS BRAVASSA. Oh, my dear, you quite divided the applause, despite it being for Miss Snevellicci—

NICHOLAS. Well, I'm sure I—(*Crummles comes to Nicholas, as Mrs. Crummles sweeps back on to the stage.*)

CRUMMLES. Johnson. Sir. This has been magnificent. Why, quite magnificent. I have not, sir, seen such a debut since the

Phenomenon herself first danced the Fairy Porcupine. (*The Infant Phenomenon curtseys and does a twirl.*) And everyone, well done. (*The Phenomenon bumps into Miss Bravassa and there is a little altercation. Lenville and Folair step forward.*)

LENVILLE. Hm. In my view, grossly over-rated.

FOLAIR. (*Leading him aside.*) Oh, come on, now, old man...

CRUMMLES. (*Taking Nicholas' arm.*) So what did you think of Miss Petowker, sir?

NICHOLAS. Oh, quite extraordinary. (*Crummles looks at Nicholas quizzically. During this a knock at the outer door and the Page-clad Miss Belvawney, out of force of habit, goes out to answer it.*) Good, is not the word. But what I did observe, additional to all her talents, was that every time she spoke, or even entered, there was quite a fearful opening and closing, in the upper boxes, of a green umbrella.

CRUMMLES. Was there? I can't say I noticed.

NICHOLAS. Yes, it was most striking. Every time she— (*Miss Snevellicci approaches bearing vast numbers of flowers, followed by Miss Ledrook, carrying the rest.*)

MISS SNEVELLICCI. Mr. Johnson.

NICHOLAS. Oh, Miss Snevellicci.

MISS SNEVELLICCI. Mr. Johnson, I—(*But even Miss Snevellicci is interrupted by the entrance of Mrs. Crummles.*)

MRS. CRUMMLES. So, are you *all* deaf?

CRUMMLES. Why, Mrs. Crummles, what's the matter?

MRS. CRUMMLES. What's the matter? The audience is what's the matter, the great Portsmouth public is the matter, they are calling for an encore from the shepherdesses, they're insisting Miss Petowker does another dance, they're shrieking out for anything from Mr. Johnson, there is a concerted move to rip the cupids and the muses from the lower boxes if Miss Snevellicci doesn't—

CRUMMLES. Then, come, let's return! Come, come, at once!

MRS. CRUMMLES. If you'd all be so kind. (*The Company running back on, as Miss Belvawney appears.*)

MISS BELVAWNEY. Psst, Mr. Johnson.

NICHOLAS. Yes?

MISS BELVAWNEY. There's someone here to see you.

139

NICHOLAS. But—

MISS BELVAWNEY. He says it's very urgent.

NICHOLAS. But I—(*Nicholas sees that Mr. Lillyvick has come in.*) Why, in the name of wonder, Mr. Lillyvick! (*Miss Belvawney scuttles across and out.*)

LILLYVICK. (*A little bow.*) Sir, I am your servant. (*He puts down a large, green umbrella.*)

NICHOLAS. And I yours. Why, there's the green umbrella!

LILLYVICK. Ah, yes, that it is. What did you think of that performance?

NICHOLAS. Your performance with the—?

LILLYVICK. What? No, I refer to Miss Petowker's.

NICHOLAS. Well, as far as I could judge, I found it most agreeable.

LILLYVICK. Agreeable? I would say, sir, it was much more than agreeable. I'd say, in fact, it was delicious.

NICHOLAS. Well, she is a clever girl.

LILLYVICK. She's a divinity. I have known divine actresses before now, sir; I used to collect the water rate at the house of a divine actress, but never in all my experience did I see a diviner creature than Miss Henrietta Petowker.

NICHOLAS. Well, yes—

LILLYVICK. (*Grasping Nicholas's arm.*) A bachelor's a miserable wretch, sir.

NICHOLAS. Is he?

LILLYVICK. I have been one nigh on sixty years. I ought to know.

NICHOLAS. That's certain.

LILLYVICK. But you know that the reason, the great reason, against marriage, is expense. That's what has kept me off it, or else, lord! I might have married fifty women.

NICHOLAS. Fifty.

LILLYVICK. But, you see: the wondrous Miss Petowker earns a salary herself. (*Pause. Lillyvick leaves Nicholas's arm. He moves a step or two away and eyes Nicholas inquiringly.*)

NICHOLAS. Uh, Mr. Lillyvick, d'you mean you're going to marry Miss Petowker?

LILLYVICK. Day after tomorrow, sir.

NICHOLAS. Well . . . Mr. Lillyvick. Congratulations.

LILLYVICK. The only problem is, the family.

NICHOLAS. What family?

LILLYVICK. The Kenwigses, of course. If my niece and her husband had known a word of it before I came away, they'd have gone into fits at my feet, and never have come off 'em till I took an oath not to marry anybody, or they'd have got out a commission of lunacy, or some such dreadful thing.

NICHOLAS. Yes, they would certainly have been quite jealous.

LILLYVICK. To prevent which, we resolved to marry here, in fact, to be married from the Crummleses, old friends of Miss Petowker, and we should be most pleased if you were there for breakfast, nothing fancy, muffins, coffee, p'raps a shrimp or something for a relish . . . .

NICHOLAS. Mr. Lillyvick, I'd be delighted. And I am most happy for you both.

LILLYVICK. Most happy? Yes. Yes—I should think it *is* a pleasant life, the married one—eh?

NICHOLAS. There is no doubt about it.

LILLYVICK. Um. No doubt. Oh, yes. Yes, certainly. (*Enter Mrs. Crummles.*)

MRS. CRUMMLES. Ah, Mr. Johnson. *Here* you are.

NICHOLAS. Oh, Mrs. Crummles. (*Lillyvick slips out, as:*)

MRS. CRUMMLES. Mr. Johnson, you are called for, in the lower circle. You're demanded in the gallery, which is, in fact, quite near collapse from all the stamping. Your appearance was entrated by dear Mrs. Curdle, till she had a palpitation and was rushed off horizontal in a fly . . . Without, of course, the wish in any way to interrupt your evening—would you be so kind, sir, as to come?

NICHOLAS. Of course I will. (*Mrs. Crummles sweeps out. Nicholas turns out front to introduce the next scene.*)

Scene Fifteen

Portsmouth. Miss Snevellicci's apartments, and the Crummles' lodgings. Bare stage, but as Nicholas speaks, Miss

141

Snevellicci, Miss Petowker and Miss Ledrook enter with a chair on one side; and Folair, Lenville, Lillyvick and the rest of the Crummles' Company Men enter the other side.

NICHOLAS. And on the morning designated for the nuptial coupling of Mr. Lillyvick and Miss Petowker, the parties were assembling; with the bridegroom and his best man Tom Folair already at the Crummleses; and Miss Petowker being finally prepared at the apartments of Miss Snevellicci. (*Miss Petowker is sitting, having a sustaining glass of something.*)

MISS PETOWKER. Oh, Lillyvick! If you only knew what I am undertaking...Leaving all my friends, the friends of youthful days, for you!

MISS LEDROOK. Of course he knows it, love, and never will forget it.

MISS PETOWKER. Are you sure? You're sure that he'll remember?

MISS SNEVELLICCI. Oh, yes, I'm absolutely sure that he'll remember. (*Focus shifts to Lillyvick.*)

FOLAIR. Come, sir, cheer up, it is soon done.

LILLYVICK. What is?

FOLAIR. The tying up, the fixing of one with a wife. It is quickly o'er. Just like a hanging, what?

LILLYVICK. Like hanging?

LENVILLE. Come on, now, Tommy none of that.

FOLAIR. Yes, yes, you know, to hang oneself takes but a moment—

LILLYVICK. Do you compare, sir, do you draw a parallel— (*Folair miming a hanging.*) Between my matrimony and a hanging?

FOLAIR. (*Still miming.*) Yes, yes, the—

LILLYVICK. You say this in the house of Mr. not to mention Mrs. Crummles, who have brought up such a family, chock full of blessings and phenomena, you call their state a noose?

FOLAIR. Well, just a little joke—(*The Bridal Party has arrived.*)

MISS PETOWKER. Oh, Lillyvick.

LILLYVICK. (*Turning to Miss Petowker.*) My dear, d'you know what this, your actor friend—

MISS PETOWKER. Oh, Lillyvick... (*Lillyvick stops, realising his Bride has arrived in her full finery on her wedding morning. He embraces Miss Petowker.*)

MISS PETOWKER. Oh, Lillyvick... You will remember, won't you? Always, always, always?

LILLYVICK. Uh, remember what, my dear? (*Enter Crummles in 18th Century costume, clearly dressed as the Heavy Father, followed by the Infant Phenomenon, covered in artificial flowers, and Mrs. Crummles, as the Distraught Mother. Some "oohs" and "ahs" from the rest. Mrs. Crummles kisses Miss Petowker, and is overcome.*)

CRUMMLES. Come, stir, stir, stir! The second cock hath crow'd, the curfew bell has rung, 'tis—(*He looks at an enormous fob watch.*) Nine o'clock.

MISS PETOWKER. (*Dramatically.*) 'Tis nine o'clock, dear Lillyvick. Come, stir. (*A wedding anthem plays. Mr. Crummles takes the arm of the bride, and walks upstage with a feeble gait. The Company form into a procession, two by two: the Bridesmaids, Mrs. Crummles with the Phenomenon, the other Actresses; then Lillyvick and Folair, the other Actors, Nicholas and Smike, and, at the rear, the drunken Mr. Wagstaff. Mr. Lillyvick is having difficulty trying to imitate the dramatic gait of the Company, and in particular of Mrs. Crummles. The Company arrives at the back of the stage, forms up in two lines—the Bride and Groom now together in the middle—and they all walk forward.*)

THE ANTHEM.

How blest are they that fear the Lord
And walk in His way
For thou shalt eat the labour of thine hands
Well, well is thee and happy shalt thou be.
Thy wife shall be
The fruitful vine on the walls of thy house
Thy children like the olive branches
Growing, growing round about thy table.
Lo, thus shall the man be blest
That feareth the Lord.
Lo, thus shall the man be blest

That feareth the Lord.
(*And there is Narration as the Bride and Groom run out, the for-
mer throwing her bouquet, which is caught by Miss Snevellicci.*)
NARRATORS.

And Mr. Lillyvick and his bride departed to take the steam-
boat to Ryde, where they were to spend the next two days
in profound retirement. (*The Company beginning to disperse, leaving only Nicholas and Smike.*)

And Mr. Crummles declared his intention of keeping the
celebrations going till everything to drink was disposed of;

But Nicholas, having to play Romeo for the first time on
the ensuing evening, and anxious on account of Smike—
who would have to sustain the character of the apothecary—
contrived to slip away. (*And only Nicholas and Smike are
left.*)

Scene Sixteen

*Portsmouth and London. Bare stage. This is a double
scene, counterpointing Nicholas' rehearsal of Smike as the
Apothecary with Ralph's dealings in London. There is an
overlap between each scene, so Smike and Nicholas don't
go out until the next little sequence is underway, and visa
versa. First, Nicholas and Smike; and, during it, Ralph
and Noggs enter. Nicholas has a copy of* Romeo and
Juliet *with him.*

NICHOLAS. (*Prompting.*) Who calls so loud?
SMIKE. Who calls so loud.
NICHOLAS.
Come hither, man. I see that thou art poor.
Hold, there is forty ducats. Let me have
A dram of poison. Such soon-speeding gear
As will disperse itself through all the veins
That the life-weary taker may fall dead,

144

And that the trunk may be discharged of breath
As violently as hasty powder fired
Doth hurry from the fatal cannon's womb.
(*Pause. Prompting.*)
Such mortal drugs I have—
SMIKE.
Such mortal drugs I have . . .
NICHOLAS.
But Mantua's law—
SMIKE.
But Mantua's law . . . .
Is death to any—one who utters them.
NOGGS. Are you at home?
RALPH. I'm not.
NOGGS. You're sure?
RALPH. Of course I'm sure.
NOGGS. Well, they're downstairs.
RALPH. Who are?
NOGGS. Two gentlemen.
RALPH. You didn't tell me.
NOGGS. Didn't ask. Ah, here they are. (*Enter Sir Matthew Pupker and Mr. Bonney. Noggs remains in the background.*)
RALPH. Sir Matthew Bonney. What can I—
BONNEY. Look, Nickleby. This matter, your investment in our company—
RALPH. Yes, yes. I have resolved to realise my capital.
BONNEY. But, Nickleby—withdrawal of a sum of that proportion, now—nine thousand?
RALPH. Ten.
BONNEY. At this stage, when the stock's still going up—
RALPH. Will make the price fall. Yes, I know.
BONNEY. The bubble—bursts!
RALPH. Yes, certainly. But I have need of it.
SIR MATTHEW. Now, Nickleby. . . .
RALPH. Sir Matthew?
SIR MATTHEW. Have you not considered this, this matter, who's involved? The highest level? Have you no thought for your country?
RALPH. I have thought of it, my country, to the same extent as

145

you have, sir. Good day. (*Sir Matthew looks at Bonney, who shrugs apologetically. Sir Matthew, with a huge gesture of rage and frustration, storms out followed by Bonney. Ralph to Noggs.*) My hat and stick.

NOGGS. Your hat and stick.

RALPH. Well, then? Don't stand, repeating what I've said. You're not a parrot.

NOGGS. Wish I was.

RALPH. Well, so do I. Then I could wring your neck. And then I would be done with you. (*Ralph strides out. Noggs stands there for a few moments, as Smike and Nicholas re-enter.*)

NICHOLAS.

> Art thou so bare and full of wretchedness,
> And fearest to die? Famine is in thy cheeks,
> Need and oppression starveth in thy eyes,
> Contempt and beggary hangs upon thy back:
> The world is not thy friend, nor the world's law;
> The world affords no law to make thee rich;
> Then be not poor, but break it, and take this.
> (*Pause. Prompting.*)
> My poverty—

SMIKE.

> My poverty . . . .

MRS. NICKLEBY. (*Off.*) Kate. Kate, my dear.

NICHOLAS.

> But not my will—

KATE. (*Off.*) Mama?

SMIKE.

> But not my will—consents.

(*Smike and Nicholas go as Mrs. Nickleby, with Ralph, enters to Kate.*)

MRS. NICKLEBY. You are to dine, dine with your uncle, half-past six tomorrow.

KATE. Uncle, what is this?

RALPH. I have a party of—of gentlemen, to whom I am connected in some business, at my house tomorrow and your mother's promised that you shall keep house for me. I'm not much used to

146

parties; but such fooleries are often part of business—and I hope
that you won't mind obliging me.

MRS. NICKLEBY. Mind? Mind? My dear Kate, tell—

KATE. I shall be very glad, of course—but I'm afraid you'll find
me very awkward and embarrassed.

RALPH. No, oh no...Come when you like, and take a hackney
coach. I'll pay for it. Good night and, um, God bless you. (*Exit
Ralph.*)

MRS. NICKLEBY. Well, Kate. Your uncle's taken quite a fancy
to you, that is clear, and if good fortune doesn't come to you
from this, I shall be most surprised. (*Kate and Mrs. Nickleby go
out during Smike and Nicholas.*)

SMIKE.

My poverty and not—

NICHOLAS.

My will—

SMIKE.

Consents.

My poverty and not my will consents.

NICHOLAS.

I pay thy poverty and not thy will.

SMIKE.

My poverty and not my will consents.

NICHOLAS. Uh—no—(*Nicholas takes Smike out, as a Man
enters one side, and on the other, Ralph and Noggs. Noggs has a
plate of muffins, which he gives to Ralph.*)

NOGGS. He's here. I got him tea. But he's not eating it. (*Ralph
gestures to Noggs, who goes. Ralph to the Man.*)

RALPH. Sir Mulberry. (*Sir Mulberry Hawk is an elegant, though
dissipated, rake. He holds a bottle and a glass.*)

HAWK. (*Pouring a drink.*) Hm. Nickleby. Is everything
arranged.

RALPH. It is. Um—have you taken tea? (*Sir Mulberry Hawk
raises his glass, in answer.*) The gull will come?

HAWK. Lord Frederick? Of course. I told him that the evening
would be both—an entertainment, and of profit. Will it be?

RALPH. Oh, yes. For us, at least. And, for the first, I think...
there will be an attraction, for his lordship, present. For the

second, I am able to advance.... as much as he, and you, will need.
HAWK. You're sure of that?
RALPH. Oh, yes. I am prepared. (*Offering the plate.*) Look,
please, Sir Mulberry, at least... Do have a muffin. Hm? (*Enter
Smike and Nicholas. They are in costume for the performance:
Nicholas as Romeo and Smike in a grey gown as the Apothecary.*)
NICHOLAS.

There is thy gold—worse poison to men's souls,

Doing more murder in this loathsome world,

Than these poor compounds that thou mayst not sell.

I sell thee poison; thou hast sold me none.

Farewell.

(*Ralph goes. Mrs. Grudden, dressed as Juliet's Nurse, marches
across the stage.*)
MRS. GRUDDEN. Act Three! Act Three! Beginners, orchestra!
(*Nicholas and Smike smile at each other.*)
SMIKE. Who calls so loud?
NICHOLAS. Who calls so loud. (*They go out.*)

Scene Seventeen

*Ralph's drawing room, in London. A chaise longue, sur-
rounded by Men in evening dress, including Sir Mulberry
Hawk, his young friend Lord Frederick Verisopht, and his
acolytes Mr. Pluck and Mr. Pyke. On another chair sits
the elderly Colonel Chowser, near to him stand the Honourable Mr. Snobb and a Makeweight. A Flunkey is in
attendance. Ralph enters with Kate.*

RALPH. Gentlemen. My niece, Miss Nickleby. (*Kate notices
they're all men.*)
VERISOPHT. Eh. What the devil.
PYKE. (*To Pluck.*) Hm ... Hm.
RALPH. My niece, my lord. Kate, Lord Frederick Verisopht.
VERISOPHT. (*Coming forward.*) Well, then me ears did not
deceive me, and it's not a waxwork. How d'ye do, Miss Nickleby.
(*Kate curtseys.*)

PYKE. (*Coming forward.*) Now, don't you leave me out, now, Nickleby.

RALPH. And this is Mr. Pyke.

PLUCK. Nor me.

RALPH. And Mr. Pluck, my dear. (*Kate curtseys again. Snobb stands.*) And the Honourable Mr. Snobb, and (*Chowser getting to his feet, not without difficulty.*) this is Colonel Chowser. (*The Makeweight obviously isn't going to be introduced, but takes advantage of the situation to go and get another drink from the Flunkey.*)

CHOWSER. Pleased. So very. Pleased. (*A slight hiatus, broken as Sir Mulberry Hawk, in one assured movement, takes the Makeweight's glass of wine, Kate's arm, and everyone's attention.*)

HAWK. Miss Nickleby, forgive us. Let me sit you down.

KATE. Why, sir I—

HAWK. (*Gliding Kate to the chaise.*) And, as I'm left out, damn you, Nickleby, I'll do the offices myself. (*Kate sits.*) Hawk, Miss Nickleby, and at your service. (*Hawk gives Kate the glass of wine.*)

KATE. Why, thank you, sir.

RALPH. (*To explain to Kate.*) Sir Mulberry. (*Verisopht to Ralph.*)

VERISOPHT. An unexpected pleasure, Nickleby. Indeed, one might say, it'd almost warrant the addition of an extra two and a half percent.

HAWK. (*Turns to Pluck.*) Eh, Nickleby should take the hint, and tack it on to the other five-and-twenty, and give me half for the advice. (*Pluck and Pyke laugh uproariously as Verisopht comes to stand on the other side of Kate's chair from Hawk.*)

VERISOPHT. Well, certainly, if he'll see to it you're not monopolising dear Miss Nickleby all night, Sir Mulberry.

RALPH. (*Lightly, as he goes to the Flunkey.*) Well, my lord, he does have a tolerable share of everything you lay claim to.

VERISOPHT. Gad, so he has. Devil take me, sometimes, if I know who's master in me own house. But I swear... I'll cut him off with but a shilling, if he—

HAWK. Sir, when you're at your last shilling, I'll be cutting you. While here is poor Miss Nickleby who's doubtless bored to tears with all this talk of discount, and hoping that some gallant fellow'll make love to her. Now, ain't that so, Miss Nickleby?

KATE. No, sir, indeed. . . .

HAWK. In fact, I'll hold you, any of you, fifty pounds, that Miss Nickleby can't look me in the face, and then deny that she was hoping so. (*To Lord Frederick Verisopht.*) My Lord?

KATE. Oh, sir. . . .

VERISOPHT. Well, why not? Done! Within a minute.

HAWK. Done. Now, Mr. Snobb, you'll take the stakes, and keep the time?

SNOBB. (*Coming to them.*) Of course. (*The Gentlemen produce money. Kate standing and going to Ralph.*)

PYKE. That's fifty pounds. . . .

CHOWSER. (*Unable to get up, pulling at Pluck.*) Hey, you, sir, pass me bet. . . .

KATE. Uncle, please. . . . please, stop them making me the subject of a bet.

RALPH. Oh, my dear . . . It's done in a moment, and there's nothing in it. . . . If the gentlemen insist—

SNOBB. One—minute! (*Hawk comes and takes Kate's hand, and leads her back to the chaise.*)

HAWK. I don't insist on it. That is, I don't insist that she denies, for even if I lose, it's worth it just to see her eyes, which seem to love the carpeting so much.

VERISOPHT. That's true. It's just too bad of you, Miss Nickleby.

PYKE. Too cruel.

PLUCK. Quite horrid cruel.

SNOBB. The lady can't deny that she was hoping for a gentleman to—um—within a minute . . . (*45 second pause.*)

HAWK. How goes it, Snobb?

SNOBB. Fifteen seconds left.

VERISOPHT. Won't you, for me, Miss Nickleby, just make one effort. . . .

HAWK. Oh, not a chance, my lord. Miss Nickleby and I understand each other very well.

SNOBB. Six, five, four, three. . . . (*Kate, outraged, looks Sir Mulberry straight in the eye. Pause. Then she breaks, stands, and runs to the side of the room.*)

HAWK. Capital. That's a girl of spirit, and we'll drink to her health. (*Hawk nods to the Flunkey, who passes round drinks as Hawk collects his winnings.*)

PYKE. Oh, yes, we will.

PLUCK. Most definitely.

PYKE. Many times.

RALPH. But, perhaps, sirs, now the sport is over, you would care to drink it over dinner.

HAWK. Well, certainly. (*Pyke and Pluck dislodge Chowser from his chair. Lord Verisopht to Kate.*)

VERISOPHT. (*Offering his arm.*) Miss Nickleby....

KATE. No, no....

RALPH. (*Gesturing the Company out.*) I'm sure Miss Nickleby will join us in a moment. When she has, composed herself.

VERISOPHT. But, Nickleby—

RALPH. I'm sure she will be down directly. Please, please, gentlemen. (*The Company leaves. Ralph is the last to go and Kate goes to him.*)

KATE. Please, uncle, don't—

RALPH. My dear. We are connected. And I can't afford...What is it, after all? We all have challenges. And this is one of yours. (*Ralph goes out. Kate is left there. Enter a heavily edited section of Act Three, Scene Five of* Romeo and Juliet, *Crummles as Capulet, Mrs. Crummles as Lady Capulet, Miss Snevellicci as Juliet and Mrs. Grudden as the Nurse. This scene is played around Kate.*)

CAPULET.

How? Will she none? Does she not give us thanks?
Is she not proud? Doth she not count her blest,
Unworthy as she is, that we have wrought
So worthy a gentleman to be her bride?

JULIET.

Proud I can never be of what I hate.

CAPULET.

God's bread! It makes me mad.
Day, night; hour, tide, time; work, play;
To have her matched; and having now provided
A gentleman of noble parentage,

To answer "I'll not wed. I cannot love;
I am too young, I pray you pardon me."!
Graze where you will, you shall not house with me.
Nor what is mine shall never do thee good.
(*Exit Capulet.*)
JULIET.
Is there no pity sitting in the clouds
That sees into the bottom of my grief?
Oh, sweet mother, cast me not away!
LADY CAPULET.
Talk not to me, for I'll not speak a word.
(*Exit Lady Capulet, Juliet and the Nurse. Re-enter Hawk.*)
HAWK. Yes, capital.
KATE. Oh, sir. . . .
HAWK. What a delightful studiousness. Was it real, now, or
only to display the eyelashes? Why did I speak and destroy such
a pretty picture?
KATE. Then please, be silent, sir. (*Hawk goes and sits next to
Kate.*)
HAWK. No, don't. Upon my life, you mustn't treat me like
this, dear Miss Nickleby. I'm such a slave of yours.
KATE. I wish, sir . . . You must understand, that your behav-
iour. . . .
HAWK. Come on, now, be more natural, Miss Nickleby, more
natural, please. . . . (*Kate looks at him. Then she stands quickly.
Hawk catches her skirt.*) A bit more natural, eh?
KATE. Oh, sir. Please. Instantly! Please let me go at once.
HAWK. Not for the world, Miss Nickleby. . . . (*Ralph has
entered.*)
RALPH. What's this? (*Hawk looks round. He sees Ralph, lets
Kate go, sits down and crosses his legs. Kate gestures vaguely.*)
(*To Hawk, gesturing towards the door.*) Your way lies there,
sir. (*Pause. Ralph shaking.*)
HAWK. (*Furious.*) Do you *know* me, you madman?
RALPH. Well. (*Pause.*)
KATE. (*In tears.*) Please, uncle. Let me go.
RALPH. Yes. Yes, of course. I'll take you to your carriage pres-
ently. (*Ralph takes Kate's arm.*) But just one word. I didn't

know it would be so; it was impossible for me to foresee it. (*Kate looking at Ralph. Ralph looking over her shoulder at Hawk.*) You have done no wrong. (*Kate goes out.*)

HAWK. Hm. You want the lord. Your pretty niece an "entertainment" for that drunken boy downstairs. (*He turns to Ralph.*) And if *he'd* come up here instead of me, you would have been a bit more blind, and deaf, and a deal less flourishing than you have been? (*Pause.*) Who brought him to you first? Without me, could you wind him in your net?

RALPH. That net's a large one, and it's rather full. Take care that it chokes no-one in its meshes.

HAWK. Oh—

RALPH. I tell you this. That if I brought her here, as a matter of business—

HAWK. Oh, yes, well, that's the word—

RALPH. (*Interrupts.*) Because I thought she might make some impression on the silly youth that you are leading into ruin, I knew, knowing him, that he'd respect her sex, and conduct. But I did not envisage I'd subject the girl to the licentiousness of a hand like you. And now we understand each other. Hm?

HAWK. Especially, of course, as there was nothing you could gain by it.

RALPH. Exactly so. (*Enter Lord Frederick Verisopht.*)

VERISOPHT. So, there you are, the both of you. Now, are we not to dine? And do some business too?

RALPH. (*Deliberately.*) Of course, my lord. We'll dine. But business first. Two months to pay. At interest of twenty-five percent. Those are the terms, what sum had you in mind?

VERISOPHT. Oh, five—or ten?

HAWK. Say, ten.

RALPH. Ten thousand pounds. Now, gentlemen, I'll join you very soon. (*Hawk and Verisopht go out one way, Ralph another. Two Crummles stage-hands run in with flats, which they set up as if the prompt side wing of our theatre was the audience of the Portsmouth theatre. Nicholas, as Romeo, walks on to "stage"— facing off our stage. In the Portsmouth wings, downstage in our theatre, are Master Crummles, waiting to enter as Balthazar, and Smike, waiting to go on as the Apothecary. Smike is concentrat-*

ing very hard, mumbling through his lines.)
ROMEO.

> If I may trust the flattering truth of sleep,
> My dreams presage some joyful news at hand.
> (*"Enter" Balthazar.*)
> News from Verona! How fares Juliet?
> For nothing can be ill if she be well.

BALTHAZAR.

> Then she is well, and nothing can be ill.
> Her body sleeps in Capel's monument,
> And her immortal part with angels lives.

ROMEO.

> Is it e'en so? Then I defy you, stars!
> Thou knowest my lodgings. Get me ink and paper
> And hire post-horses. I'll be with you straight.
> (*Exit Balthazar.*)
> Well, Juliet, I will lie with thee tonight.
> Let's see for means. O mischief, thou art swift
> To enter in the thoughts of desperate men!
> I do remember an apothecary,
> And hereabouts 'a dwells, which late I noted
> In tatt'red weeds, with overwhelming brows,
> Culling of simples. This should be the house.
> What, ho! Apothecary!
> (*Pause. Smike has been concentrating so hard, he's missed his cue. Nicholas repeats.*)
> What, ho! Apothecary!
> (*Smike rushes on, and bellows out.*)

APOTHECARY.

> WHO CALLS SO LOUD?

(*And Nicholas leads him away, as Ralph brings Kate downstage.*)

KATE. And as the door of her carriage was closed, a comb fell from Kate's hair, close to uncle's feet; and as he picked it up and returned it into her hand, the light from a neighbouring lamp shone upon her face. (*Ralph is lit.*)

RALPH. The lock of hair that had escaped and curled loosely over her brow, the traces of tears yet scarcely dry, the flushed cheek, the look of sorrow, all fired some dormant train of recollection in the old man's breast; and the face of his dead brother seemed present before him, with the very look it wore on some occasion of boyish grief, of which every minute circumstance flashed upon his mind, with the distinctness of a scene of yesterday. (*And Newman Noggs appears.*)

NOGGS. And Ralph Nickleby, who was proof against all appeals of blood and kindred—who was steeled against every tale of sorrow and distress—staggered while he looked, and reeled back into the house, as a man who had seen a spirit from a world beyond the grave. (*Darkness.*)

Scene Eighteen

The stage of the Portsmouth Theatre. A tatty, Crummlesian set for the last scene of Romeo *and* Juliet. *Downstage, Miss Snevellicci—as Juliet—and Mr. Lenville—as Tybalt—lie on couches, as if dead. Upstage, a badly painted cut-out of two arches, and behind that, a backcloth of Verona.*

A note on this scene: There is much opportunity here, in addition to the written jokes, for merriment. In the original production, one of the best visual jokes was an increasing pile of mattocks, irons, torches and swords that were dumped, during the first half of the scene, downstage, between the two couches, and over which people had to walk. There are many other opportunities for making the point that the Crummles Company are a troupe of not-very-good actors and actresses who have to rehearse plays very quickly, and therefore do not always get everything sorted out beforehand. Enter Mr. Bane as Paris and Miss Belvawney as his Page.

PARIS.
Give me thy torch. Do as I bid thee, go.
PAGE. (*Aside.*)

I am almost afraid to stand alone
Here in the churchyard; yet I will adventure.
PARIS.
Sweet flower, with flowers thy bridal bed I strew
Which with sweet water nightly I will dew;
(*The Page whistles.*)
The boy gives warning something doth approach.
(*Paris retires. Enter Nicholas as Romeo, and Master Crummles as Balthazar, with a mattock and a crow of iron.*)
iron.)
ROMEO.
Give me that mattock and the wrenching iron.
Give me the light. Therefore hence, be gone.
Live, and be prosperous, and farewell, good fellow.
BALTHAZAR.
(*Aside.*) For all this same, I'll hide me hereabout.
His looks I fear, and his intents I doubt.
(*Balthazar retires. Romeo, opening the tomb.*)
ROMEO.
Thou detestable maw, thou womb of death,
Gorged with the dearest morsel of the earth.
(*Paris strides forward.*)
PARIS.
Stop thy unhallowed toil, vile Montague!
Condemned villain, I do apprehend thee.
ROMEO.
Good gentle youth, tempt not a desperate man,
By urging me to fury. O, be gone!
PARIS.
I apprehend thee for a felon here.
ROMEO.
Wilt thou provoke me! Then, have at thee, boy!
PARIS' PAGE.
O, lord, they fight! I will go call the watch.
(*Paris falls.*)
PARIS.
Oh, I am slain! If thou be merciful,

Open the tomb, and lay me with Juliet.
(*He shuts his eyes.*)
ROMEO.

In faith I will. Let me peruse thy face.
Mercutio's kinsman, noble County Paris!
(*Pulling Paris' body into the tomb.*)
I'll bury thee in a triumphant grave.
A grave? Oh, no, a lanthorn, slaughtered youth,
(*Dropping Paris' body and running to Juliet.*)
For here lies Juliet, and her beauty makes
This vault a feasting presence full of light.
Tybalt, liest thou there in thy bloody sheet?
Why art thou yet so fair? Shall I believe
That unsubstantial death is amorous.
For fear of that I still will stay with thee
With worms that are thy chambermaids. O, here
Will I set up my ever lasting rest.
Here's to my love! Thus with a kiss I die.
(*He drinks the poison and kisses Juliet. Outside the tomb,
enter Mr. Fluggers as Friar Lawrence. He carries a crow and
spade.*)
FRIAR.

St. Francis be my speed! How now! Who's there!
BALTHAZAR.

Here's one, a friend, and one that knows you well.
FRIAR.

Alack, alack, what blood is this which stains
The stony entrance of this sepulchre?
BALTHAZAR.

Then what I took to be a dream is true,
And—further horror—I did hear him speak
Of some fell liquor that with venomous speed
Would him to death's black bosom swift despatch.
FRIAR.

Then all is lost! Juliet still sleeps—
What unkind hour is guilty of this chance!
The watch approaches, we must fast away;

Come, come, good friend, we dare no longer stay.
(*The Friar and Balthazar run out. In the tomb, Juliet wakes.*)
JULIET.
What's here? A cup, closed in my true love's hand?
Poison, I see, hath been his timeless end.
Oh, churl! Drunk all, and left no friendly drop
To help me after? What, and Paris too?
(*Juliet goes to Paris's body.*)
Oh, County, that would take my maidenhead:
Lie here, thy dagger rests in Juliet's bed.
(*Juliet about to stab herself with Paris's dagger. Romeo sits up.*)
ROMEO.
Hold, hold! I live!
JULIET.
What, Romeo, not dead?
ROMEO.
The pothac's poison coursed throughout my veins
A dizzy drowsiness which I mistook
For that numb torpor which doth presage death,
But in an instant it has passed. What, Juliet?
JULIET.
Oh, Romeo, thou starts. I am not dead
For I too drank a draught of fluid that
Had longer but the same benign effect!
(*The Watchman, played by Mr. Pailey, the comic country-man, appears.*)
WATCHMAN.
What's there? Who's that within! What's there! What ho!
Come, lights! Come, malting hooks! Look! Here! Look ho!
ROMEO.
We are approached.
(*Enter the Prince, played by Mr. Wagstaff, the drunken, virtuous old man. Falling to his knee.*)
WATCHMAN.
Good morrow, noble Prince.

PRINCE.

What calls our person from our morning rest?

(*He goes into the tomb. The Watchman stands. Enter Crummles as Capulet.*)

CAPULET.

What should it be, that is so shrieked abroad?

(*He goes into the tomb. Enter Mrs. Crummles as Lady Capulet, and Juliet's Little Brother, played by Master P. Crummles, and Peter, played by Mr. Folair.*)

LADY CAPULET.

What fear is this which startles in our ears?

(*They go into the tomb.*)

PRINCE.

Ah, Romeo!

JULIET'S BROTHER.

Oh, sister!

LADY CAUPLET.

Paris!

PETER.

Slain!

CAPULET.

What strange reversal hath this morning brought,
With Romeo returned—

LADY CAPULET.

He having fled,
Dead Juliet alive,

CAPULET.

Quick Paris dead.

(*Paris sits up.*)

PARIS.

Not dead so much as stunned, for Romeo's blow
Deflected from my heart, did but a moment give
The appearance and accoutrements of death.

JULIET.

As with my potion!

ROMEO.

And the pothac's draught!

159

(*Enter the irascible Mr. Blightey as Montague, Mrs. Lenville as Lady Montague, Miss Gazingi as an Attendant, and the Phenomenon as Romeo's Little Sister.*)

MONTAGUE.

What's this? The people cry of blackest death,

LADY MONTAGUE.

Some others of deliverance divine,

MONTAGUE.

Talk both of grief and joy's on every breath:

(*Enter Miss Ledrook as Rosaline.*)

ROSALINE.

Oh Romeo!

ROMEO.

        Good heavens.

(*To Juliet.*)

          Rosaline.

(*Pause. Mr. Wagstaff's attention has wandered. Mrs. Grudden's head appears from the prompt corner.*)

MRS. GRUDDEN. But mourning—

PRINCE.

But mourning flowers now adorn a festival,

And merry peals o'ertake the tolls of funeral.

ROMEO.

'Tis true, our joy demands a cheerful bell:

Oh, Mother, Father, Sister mine as well!

(*Romeo embraces his Little Sister. Pause. Someone nudges Mr. Wagstaff.*)

PRINCE.

Who's there?

(*Enter the Friar, who throws himself to the ground before the Prince.*)

FRIAR.

        Dread sovereign, in guilty flight

I did attempt to 'scape your wrathful judgement.

But conscience stayed my steps, and turned them round,

And, penitent, I here abase myself.

PRINCE.

What, penitent? There is no crime, stand, see!

160

All those in chains of death are unbound, free.
FRIAR.
What joy! Then further tidings I must tell,
For on my hurried passage, I did meet
Another whom the jaws of death let go:
See, here, Prince, is your kin, Mercutio!
(*Enter Mr. Hetherington, the swaggerer, as Mercutio, and Miss Bravassa, dressed as a man, as Benvolio.*)
CAPULET.
Mercutio! Recover'd!
MERCUTIO.
Ay, sirs, ay,
For though thought dead, and bourn for balming up
My friend Benvolio observed a breath
Of slight proportion on my countenance
And I was taken to a nearby town,
Where I was cured by surgeons of renown.
FRIAR.
And further news comes with him. Speak, Benvolio!
(*Pause. Folair gestures to Miss Bravassa, who shrugs, and points at Mr. Wagstaff.*)
MRS. GRUDDEN. (*Appearing again.*) Yes, yes—
PRINCE.
Yes, yes, Benvolio, speak.
BENVOLIO.
I shall, my lord,
But 'tis a tale I fear will try thy patience,
But I swear 'tis true. My friends know, oft
In their society have I been told
In jest, I am too gentle for our revels,
And almost feminine in countenance,
With not a hair of manhood on my chin.
Oft has it been so said; and I have laughed,
And spoken gruff, and slapped my thigh, to counter it.
But now deception's o'er, and I confess
That from this same near town I once did flee,
Pursuant of a love that fate denied,
And so t'effect my passage, took myself

161

The form and outward clothing of that sex
To which my love but not myself belongs.
(*Benvolio reaches up, takes off his cap, and lets fall her long hair.*)
From nature let deceit no more disbar:
Benvolio become Benvolia!
PARIS.
Ah me.
CAPULET.
    Ah?
LADY CAPULET.
        You?
BENVOLIA.
           Ay, sirs, 'tis he,
Who thus from fell disguise releases me.
PRINCE.
So everything is done—
(*Enter Paris' Page, followed by Balthazar and the Apothecary.*)
PAGE.
        What Paris? Oh!
Hath sweet concord o'ertaken—
BALTHAZAR.
        Romeo!
Upon the road, in flight, I did perchance
To come upon this wizened, withered man,
Who hobbling was along the way from Mantua,
And asked where he might find a desperate man
Who might have bought a deathly liquid from him.
From your description I resolved it was
That self-same wretch from whom you bought the dram
Of poison in that self-same town. I asked
What was his purpose, and he told me straight,
The darkness, and his age, and dread infirmity,
Had caused him to prepare not poison, but
An harmless cordial, of sharp effect
But of no lasting peril.

(*Balthazar notices everything else.*)
Oh. What's this?
ROMEO.

Good Balthazar, all matters are resolved,
And good apothecary, thy mischance
Has proved the most enduring, happy circumstance.
PRINCE.

And now at last may tocsin loudly ring?
And tabor sound? And minstrels sweetly sing?
ROMEO.

Yes, yes. All's concluded. Everything is done.
(*The Company is leaving the tomb, when Lady Capulet
runs to the corse of Tybalt, and cradles it in her arms.*)
LADY CAPULET.

But what of Tybalt? Tybalt, still lies locked
Within the dread embrace of dreader death.
CAPULET.

Why, come, dear wife, a half an hour ago,
We'd thought a half-a-dozen kin were slain.
Let grievance cease, let Tybalt's bones remain.
LADY CAPULET.

Yes, let it be.
(*She drops Tybalt back on the slab. This gesture hurts Mr.
Lenville's head.*)
Let Tybalt lie still there.
And to a merry dance let us repair.
PRINCE.

A blooming peace this morning with it brings,
The sun for happiness shines forth his head,
Go hence, to have more talk of happy things,
All shall be pardoned, and none punished.
For never was a story better set
Than this of Romeo and his Juliet.
(*Blackout. The Crummles Company form up for their curtain
call, except for Mrs. Crummles, and the doubles—if they are in
the Company—of Squeers, Young Wackford and Brooker, who
have a quick change. The lights come up, for the Company's cur-*)

*tain call. Then they go down again, and Mrs. Crummles enters as
Britannia, with helmet and union flag. The lights come up, and
with them, the music of the Crummles' closing song.*)
MRS. CRUMMLES.
    England, arise: *
    Join in the chorus!
    It is a new-made song you should be singing.
    See in the skies,
    Fluttering before us,
    What the bright bird of peace is bringing.
CRUMMLES COMPANY.
    See upon our smiling land,
    Where the wealths of nations stand,
    Where Prosperity and Industry walk ever hand in hand.
    Where so many blessings crowd,
    'Tis our duty to be proud:
    Up and answer, English yeomen, sing it joyfully aloud!
    Evermore upon our country,
    God will pour his rich increase:
    And victorious in war shall be made glorious in peace.
(*And now the Crummles' closing song becomes our closing
song, and the rest of our Company enter: Kate, Mrs. Nickleby,
Mr. and Mrs. Lillyvick; Squeers, Young Wackford and one or
more Dotheboys Hall Boys; The Mantalinis; available Kenwigs;
Sir Matthew Pupker, Hawk, Verisopht and Ralph, representing
High Society; Mr. Crowl, Noggs and the ragged beggar Brooker
representing the low. And in the middle, Nicholas and Smike,
triumphant; as the Song moves to its climax.*)
WHOLE COMPANY.
    See each one do what he can
    To further God's almighty plan:
    The benificence of heaven help the skilfulness of man.

    Every garner filled with grain,
    Every meadow blest with rain,

---

* See special note on copyright page.

Rich and fertile is the golden corn that bears and bears
    again.

Where so many blessings crowd,
Tis our duty to be proud:
Up and answer, English yeomen, sing it joyfully aloud!

Evermore upon our country
God will pour his rich increase:
And victorious in war shall be made glorious in peace.

(*And the lights fade finally on the tableau.*)

END OF PART ONE.

CASTING NOTES

One of the central concepts of *Nicholas Nickleby* was that the acting company were in collective possession of an entire story, which they were then to tell to an audience. True, certain actors would tell more of the story than some others; but everybody knew it, how it started and how it ended, and the company as a whole was, in one sense, the single character of the play. Everybody took part in the narration (it is important, for example, that in the two narration sequences that open the plays, everybody should have at least one line) and actors not playing a named part would, when not changing or preparing for an entrance, sit or stand round, on the set, watching their story unfold.

For this reason, there are no "extras" in *Nicholas Nickleby.* All the available performers should take part in the collective, narrative sequences; and it is no matter if, for example, Fanny Squeers turns up as a Milliner at the Mantalinis, or Ralph Nickleby as a blind beggar in the London street scenes of Part Two. Indeed, in the Dotheboys Hall sections, it is vital that the Boys are played by adult performers, who reappear in other guises in the rest of the play (in the original production, Mr. Snawley sent his wretched children off to Dotheboys' Hall in Act One Scene Six, and reappeared playing the Boy Tomkins in Scene Ten). Because of the sexual break-down of the original company, actors put on skirts and bonnets to supplement the Milliners in Part One and the guests at Mrs. Kenwigs' confinement in Part Two; and actresses appeared as some of the Boys at Mr. Squeers' loathsome Academy. And, in some scenes where large numbers of specific types of people were felt to be useful, everybody available was roped in: every free actor played a member of Mr Pugstyles' deputation in Part One, and every actor not in the Crummles Theatre Company attended Ralph's dinner party at the end of Act Two; in Part Two, almost the entire company entered the Saracens' Head coffee room in Act Two Scene One; and the majority were involved as walls, doors, railings, bodies and revellers in the long sequence leading up to Ralph's suicide.

The specific casting, too, will depend on what talents are available. To give an idea of the breadth of our company, there is the example of Mr Folair, the pantomimist, who in the original run of the play was doubled with Young Wackford Squeers; in the New York revival, he was played by the actor whose other main part was the down-and-out Brooker. The opera singers were chosen because they could sing (one of them also played Ralph Nickleby); the Infant Phenomenon started off doubling with Tilda Price, and ended up being played by the actress who also performed Morleena Kenwigs, Snawley Minor and Miss La Creevy's maid Hannah. There is no need for the Fanny Squeers actress also to play Miss Snevellicci and Peg Sliderskew (though it is a wonderful triple for an actress), nor even for every performer to have at least two speaking parts (although it is preferable, and we managed it with everyone except the actor playing Nicholas himself). The cast list given here (which is of the New York revival) is thus merely one of many possible combinations.

COSTUME NOTES

A quick glance down the cast list will demonstrate why it is impossible to give a detailed costume plot; but I hope that these notes may be helpful in assembling the immense array of costumes needed for *Nicholas Nickleby*. The first point is that everybody will need some kind of basic, neutral costume for narration, crowd-work and so on: for many of the shorter parts, the "costume" will consist of the addition of a scarf, jacket, hat or bonnet to this basic outfit. The second general point is that most people in early Victorian England possessed very few clothes indeed. Newman Noggs' rusty, ill-fitting suit is probably worn every day of the year. When characters *do* appear in different costumes (Miss Petowker in her wedding-dress, Noggs himself in his evening clothes near the end of Part Two) it is thus a highly significant matter. And, third, it should be remembered that Nicholas Nickleby is set in *very* early Victorian England; many of the characters (particularly the older ones) will look more Regency than what we generally think of as Victorian: Sir Mulberry Hawk and his entourage, for instance, will look more eighteenth than nineteenth century, with their striped trousers, elegant whiskers and flashy waistcoats.

Beyond that, there are some specific points. Mrs. Nickleby, Nicholas and Kate will be in mourning black throughout, as will be Madeline Bray after the death of her father. Men's hats vary from flat (Squeers and Brooker) to quite tall (Nicholas and Noggs). The three Cheerybles should be dressed in good, solid and comfortable cloth (and all the same colour); the Kenwigs' party should be alive with colour, though not as dazzling as the full finery of the Crummles' theatre company. The Milliners will wear basic white, greyed by the filthy London streets; the two little Snawleys and Belling wear neat grey trousers, short black jackets, white blouses and caps. At Dotheboys

Hall we see that the Boys must have once worn something similar, now they are in rags and tatters, far too small, and supplemented by bits and pieces against the bitter cold (Smike, who has been there longest, is the most ragged). In the original production, the Gentleman Next Door wore combinations, yellow slippers and a nightcap; Kate changed into a dressy, black-silk evening-gown for Ralph's dinner party and the opera; and Ralph himself, Mr. Mantalini and Miss LaCreevy were among the many characters whose costumes were faithful reproductions of the detailed descriptions given of them in the original novel.

STAGING NOTES

The set for Nicholas Nickleby, designed by John Napier and Dermot Hayes, consisted of an extremely complex wooden structure, created to fit the peculiar dimensions of the Aldwych Theatre in London (Nickleby's Broadway home, the Plymouth theatre, was chosen because of its similarity to the Aldwych). It is unlikely that future producers will wish accurately to reproduce all of the characteristics of the Napier/Hayes set, but I describe it here in case some of its elements can be included.

The set was two-tier; the ground level consisted of a shallow wooden rake, with a trap-door downstage centre and a walkway running out through the orchestra from the middle of the front of the stage. Upstage right-centre was a low truck that could run, on a trajectory nearly at right-angles to the front of the stage, down to front centre. Off left was a higher and larger truck that could also run to centre stage, at an acuter angle, and which could fit flush behind the smaller truck, if necessary, to form a two-tier platform that filled most of the downstage area. The small truck and the large truck could enter and be used separately as well; and the large truck could also split in half, and its downstage half could be wheeled on on its own.

The upper tier of the set was, in essence, an asymmetrical complex of platforms and walkways that surrounded the main acting area, and extended round the front of the mezzanine. On each side, two storeys of small platforms, connected by steps and ladders, rose up from the floor; these structures were connected, at the back of the stage, by an angular bridge (roughly above the resting-place of the small truck), a central support system, and another, smaller bridge (roughly above the resting-place of the large truck). Behind the central support structure between the bridges was a wooden ramp, heading upstage, which led to a staircase facing back downstage, connecting the ramp

170

with floor level. The side-structures were also connected by a long, semi-circular walk-way built on to the front of the mezzanine (supported by scaffolding from the orchestra level of the auditorium).

The basic, dark-wood set was decorated with metal gates and railings, hanging ropes and elements of furniture (wooden chairs hung on pegs, waiting for use; a frequently used step-ladder hung in the middle of the central support-system). Most of the action took place on the ground-floor level, on or off the trucks; but the platforms and walkways were constantly filled with actors watching the action, or taking part in narration. The mezzanine walk-way was used in two set-piece chase sequences, and by performers in the big London scenes.

Despite the fact that most of the action of the novel takes place in rooms, no attempt was (or should be) made to represent the actuality of walls, windows and doors. There are frequent occasions, however, when door-knocking and bell-ringing are important elements of the plot. The best solution is to mime the action of knocking, or to pull on an actual bell-pull, with the actual sound being provided by performers, openly and visibly hitting the side of the structure, or ringing a handbell, to provide the effect. Thus, when Mr. Crowl arrived to interrupt the Kenwigs' party in Act Two of Part One, the actor arrived beyond an imaginary door, another actor offstage made a knocking sound, and only then did the Kenwigs become aware of Crowl's presence. Similarly, when (in Act Three of Part Two) Squeers and Peg Sliderskew communicate by knocking on a wall connecting their two rooms, the performers mimed knocking on an imaginary wall between them, in time to sound effects provided live by performers upstage.

The effectiveness of these live sound effects led the directors to conclude that there should be no recorded effects. Performers watching the action provided the wind of the North Yorkshire moors, the bird-song of the countryside, the street-sounds of London, and the hoove-sounds of the horses who transport the characters at various points in the story.

Finally, an early decision was made that it would be madness to attempt to provide specific furniture for the various ambiances of the play. There was a fixed stock of basic (but carefully-chosen) furniture, that served the purposes of the entire show. One small sofa, for example (suitably decorated and cushioned) served for the Squeers' parlour in Yorkshire, Miss La Creevy's front room in London, Sir Mulberry Hawk's elegant apartments in Regent St. and much besides: similarly, one chaise longue was rapidly transformed (at the end of Act Two of Part One) from the centre-piece of Ralph's luxurious drawing room to Juliet's slab in the Capulet Tomb in *Romeo and Juliet*. The wicker-work skips that formed the basis of Nicholas' coach to Yorkshire reappeared with the Crummles' Theatre Company; and the company's simple, brick-painted flats were used to represent the wall of Miss La Creevy's garden.

SPECIFIC STAGING

Although companies may not have the benefit of two trucks and a trap-door, it might be useful to directors to know specifically how these mechanic devices were used in the original production of *Nicholas Nickleby*. The following detailed plot is thus provided.

PART ONE

1.1 The large truck was in place for the opening of the show, and the actors were grouped on and in front of it for the opening narration. The truck was wheeled out during the initial chaos of the Nicklebys' arrival in London.

1.2 The muffin-boys, and other passers-by, left the stage via the orchestra and mezzanine walk-ways, to watch and participate in this scene from the auditorium. At the end, the muffin-boys ran back on to the stage via these walkways, and the orchestra walkway was also Noggs' entrance.

1.7 As described in the text, half the large truck formed the base of the coach to Yorkshire.

1.8 After the exit of the coach, the small truck came forward to represent Miss La Creevy's room, pre-set with an armchair (with a gaudy cloth thrown over) and a small desk and chair for Miss La Creevy herself. The truck left during Kate's conversation with Ralph at the end of the scene.

1.10 No desks or benches were provided for the Boys in this scene.

1.13 The entrance to the Boys' dormitory was deemed to be the trapdoor downstage centre. This provided entrances for Smike (at the beginning of the scene) and Fanny at the end.

1.18/ Once again, the trap was deemed to be the entrance to the
19 dormitory, and was used by Nicholas at the beginning of Scene 18, and by Mr. and Mrs. Squeers in Scene 19.

1.20 The first Mantalini scene was on a bare stage.

1.21 As soon as Madame Mantalini invites Kate to the work-room, the large truck entered to represent the showroom, (pre-set with tailors' dummies, a chaise longue and a mirror), and the clothesrails and dummies of the work-room were set up downstage right, on floor-level, by the Milliners. During Kate's final monologue, Kate left the showroom and returned to the (now empty) workroom area: the truck left on Miss Knag's "I love her, I quite love her..." line, with that lady standing at its downstage right corner.

1.22 Squeers' entrance to the beating scene was all around the mezzanine walkway, across the bridge, and down the back staircase.

2.2 The Kenwigs' crowded front parlour was pre-set on the small truck, which came forward during Mr. Crowl's introductory line, and withdraw during the last two lines of the scene.

2.5 The structure of the Mantalinis' work-room and showroom were the same as in 1.21.

2.6 The Kenwigs' truck, having remained set, came forward during the Narration starting "And Newman hastened with joyful steps..." It withdrew on the last line of the scene.

2.11 In this scene, the showroom was not on the large truck, but set on the floor. The Milliners' chase of Mr. Mantalini took place all round the mezzanine walkway; Mantalini returned to ground level via the back staircase.

2.13. Ralph's office, as described in the text, had been set on the small truck.

2.14 To represent the side-wing of the Crummles' stage, it was useful to set a small flat in our right wing.

2.18 The Crummles' *Romeo and Juliet* was performed on and in front of the large truck. Two chaise-longue, downstage, represented Juliet and Tybalt's slabs; an arch-cloth hung in front of the large-cloth, to represent the back wall of the tomb; and a back-cloth of Verona hung in front of the central bridges, behind the large truck.

PROPERTIES

ACT ONE

SCENE 2
(London Tavern)
  Bring on
  Muffin trays (Muffineers)
    Muffins (Muffineers)
  Staff (Flunkey)
  Truncheons (Policemen)
  "Resolution" (to read) (Bonney)
SCENE 3
(London Street)
  Bring on
  Letter, black bordered (Noggs)
SCENE 4
(Street; House)
  Bring on
  Paintbrush (Miss La Creevy)
  Business card (Miss La Creevy)
  Chair, for Mrs. Nickleby (Nicholas)
  Newspaper clipping (Ralph)
SCENE 5
(Coffee House: Saracen's Head)
  Set up
  Table
  Trunk
  Ledger (and money) for Squeers
  Bring on
  Newspaper (Squeers)
  Newspaper clipping (Snawley)
  Letter (Noggs)
SCENE 6
(Nicklebys' Rooms)

Bring on
Suitcase (Mrs. Nickleby)
Books (Kate)
Clothes (Kate)
SCENE 7
(Saracen's Head)
Set up
Table, set with:
eggs, ham (on plate)
Mobile truck comes on with
chairs, tables, luggage, etc. to build "coach"
Bring on
Tray (Maid), with:
jug of water
1 piece bread and butter (on plate)
Mug of milk (Squeers)
Letter (Noggs)
Whip (Coachman)
Horn (Hornblower)
SCENE 8
(Miss La Creevy's House)
Set up
Small table, with Miss La Creevy's painting equipment
Chair, on small platform (for Kate)
SCENE 9
(Dotheboys Hall: exterior; interior)
Set up
Falling snow
Bring on
Luggage (2 Snawleys; Belling)
Big chair (Phib)
Table (Phib)
Tray, with brandy, glasses and water (Phib)
Letters and documents (Squeers)
Spoon (on string around neck) (Mrs. Squeers)
Letter (in coat pocket) (Nicholas)
Glass of brandy (Noggs)
SCENE 10
(Dotheboys Hall: interior)

176

Bring on
Cane (Squeers)
Bowl of "brimstone and treacle" (Smike)
Spoon (on string around neck) (Mrs. Squeers)
Letters (in pocket) (Squeers)
SCENE 11
(Dotheboys Hall: exterior)
Bring on
Luggage (John Browdie)
SCENE 12
(Dotheboys Hall: Squeers' Parlour)
Bring on
Sofa (Boys)
Glass of wine (Squeers)
Bellings' clothes (Mrs. Squeers, for Wackford)
Knitting (Fanny)
SCENE 13
(Dotheboys Hall: Dormitory)
Bring on
Book (Nicholas)
SCENE 14
(Miss La Creevy's House)
Bring on
Luggage (Kate and Hannah)
Handkerchief (Miss La Creevy)
SCENE 15
(Dotheboys Hall: Parlour)
Set up
Table
2 chairs
Playing cards (for Nicholas)
Bring on
Settings for tea (Phib)
Plate of bread and butter (Phib)
SCENE 16
(Mrs. Nickleby's House)
Set up
2 broken chairs (Boys)
Carpet (threadbare) (Boys)

177

Bring on
Luggage (Kate's and Mrs. Nickleby's, brought on by Noggs)
Purse (Mrs. Nickleby)
SCENE 18
(Dotheboys Hall: Dormitory)
Bring on
Nicholas' book (from Scene 13) (Smike)
Candle (Nicholas)
Paper and pen (Nicholas)
SCENE 20
(Mantalinis' Breakfast Room)
Set up
Table, 2 chairs on one side
1 chair on other side
Bring on
Ralph's letter (Kate)
SCENE 21
(Mantalinis' Workroom: Downstage)
Set up
Clothesrails
Tailors' dummies
Hatboxes
Uncompleted dresses and hats
(Mantalinis' Showroom: Upstage)
Set up
Display tailors' dummies
Hatboxes
Chaise longue
Tall mirror
Coats and hats (to be tried on by Rich Daughter)
Bring on
Letter from Nicholas (Kate)
SCENE 22
(Dotheboys Hall: Schoolroom)
Bring on
Pair of steps (The Thrashing Horse) (Boys)
Long cane (Squeers)
Ropes (to tie Smike) (Boys)

178

SCENE 23
(Countryside)
  Bring on
  Lamp (John Browdie)
  Stout staff (John Browdie)
  Purse (John Browdie)
  Money, in purse (John Browdie)
SCENE 24
(Dotheboys Hall: Parlour)
  Bring on
  Letter (Fanny)

ACT TWO

SCENE 1
(Noggs' Room)
  Set up
  Armchair
  Bring on
  Fanny's letter (Noggs)
  Unlit candle (Crowl)
SCENE 2
(Kenwigs' Living Room)
  Set up
  Chairs
  Table, with
    trays, glasses, bowl of punch
  Bring on
  Hat (Mr. Lillyvick)
  "Baby" (Nicholas)
SCENE 3
(Noggs' Room)
  Set up
  Armchair
  Bring on
  Bottle and 2 glasses (Noggs)
  Fanny's letter (Nicholas)

179

SCENE 4
(Westminster; Pupker's Office)
Set up
Desk
Map of world ("impressive")
Chair
Copy of *The Times*
Bring on
Spectacles (Pugstyles)
List of questions (Pugstyles)
Lists of questions (Delegation)
SCENE 5
(Mantalinis' Workroom: Downstage)
Set up
Clothesrails
Tailors' dummies
Hatboxes
Uncompleted dresses and hats
(Mantalinis' Showroom: Upstage)
Set up
Display tailors' dummies
Hatboxes
Chaise longue
Tall mirror
Bell pull (for Mme. Mantalini)
Bring on
2 bonnets (Miss Knag, for Young Fiancee)
SCENE 6
(Noggs' Room: Downstage)
Set up
Noggs' armchair
(Kenwigs' Room: Upstage)
Bring on
Glass of brandy (Mr. Lillyvick)
Jug of water (Mr. Lillyvick)
SCENE 7
(The Nicklebys' House)
Set up
Chair (for Mrs. Nickleby)

Bring on
Fanny Squeers' letter (Ralph)
SCENE 8
(London Street)
Set up
Table (for Scene 9)
Bench (for Scene 9)
Bring on
Bundles (Nicholas and Smike)
Can (of rum and milk) (Noggs)
SCENE 9
(Inn, near Portsmouth)
Set up
2 wash tubs
Waterpump
Baggage
2 reins
    (to construct "phaeton")
Bring on
2 wooden swords (2 Crummles sons)
Baggage (2 Crummles sons)
Bag (containing script) (Crummles)
SCENE 10
(Portsmouth Theatre: Stage)
Bring on
Clothes rail (Mrs. Grudden)
Chair; Table (Mr. Bane, Mr. Hetherington)
    (for Mrs. Crummles)
Luggage (Company)
Walking stick (Mr. Folair)
List (Mrs. Grudden)
Costumes for Smike (Mrs. Grudden)
Pages of script for Nicholas (Crummles)
Suitcase (full of bottles) (Mr. Wagstaff)
Newspaper (Mr. Fluggers)
SCENE 11
(Mantalinis' Showroom)
Set up
Chair

Mirror
Clothes rail
Clothes stands (with dresses)
Tailors' dummies
Bell pull
Bring on
Business card (Scaley)
Document (Scaley)
Inventory book (Tix)
Scissors (Mantalini)

SCENE 12
(Portsmouth: Various Locations)
Bring on
Pile of sheets and towels (Miss Snevellicci)
Scrapbook (Miss Snevellicci)
Chair (for Mrs. Curdle) (Mr. Curdle)
Sheets of paper ("circulars") (Miss Snevellicci)
Theatrical poster (Crummles) (shows name of
    "Miss Petowker, Theatre Royal, Drury Lane")
Letter (Mrs. Crummles)
Luggage (for Miss Petowker) (Miss Petowker, Boys)

SCENE 13
(Ralph Nickleby's Office)
Set up
Desk
Chairs (on either side)
Cash box (on desk)
Bring on
Bills of Exchange (Mantalini)
Business card from Scaley and Tix (Noggs)
Bill, to Ralph (Scaley)
(Noggs' Room)
Set up
High stool
Ledger table, with bell and account books

SCENE 14
(Portsmouth Theatre: Wings)
Bring on
Bunches of flowers (Miss Snevellicci)

Large green umbrella (Mr. Lillyvick)

SCENE 15

(Portsmouth: Miss Snevellicci's Apartments)

Bring on

Chair for Miss Petowker (Ladies)

Glass of wine (Miss Petowker)

Enormous fob watch (Crummles)

Bridal bouquet (Miss Petowker)

SCENE 16

(Portsmouth; London)

Bring on

Copy of *Romeo and Juliet* (Nicholas)

Plate of muffins (Noggs)

Bottle and glass (Sir Mulberry Hawk)

SCENE 17

(Ralph Nickleby's Drawing Room)

Set up

Chaise longue

Chair

Bring on

Tray, with wine glasses (Flunkey)

Pound notes (Gentlemen)

Flats for *Romeo and Juliet* (Crummles' stage hands)

SCENE 18

(Portsmouth Theatre: Stage)

Set up

"Tatty" set for *Romeo and Juliet*:

   backcloth of Verona

   badly painted cutout of 2 arches

   Cup of "poison" (by Juliet's body)

Bring on

Torch (Crummles)

Mattock (Crummles)

Wrenching iron (Crummles)

Crow(bar) (Mr. Fluggers)

Spade (Mr. Fluggers)

Dagger (Mr. Bane, as Paris)

Helmet (Mrs. Crummles, as Britannia)

Union flag (Mrs. Crummles, as Britannia)

RECENT

 Releases . . .

ALBUM

MIXED COUPLES

THE CAPTIVITY
  OF PIXIE SHEDMAN

BACK IN THE RACE

THE TANTALUS

STILL LIFE

BEAUTY AND THE BEAST
  (Children's play)

THYMUS VULGARIS

LIMBO TALES (3 short plays)

THE FORMER ONE-ON-ONE
  BASKETBALL CHAMPION

THE TERRIBLE TATTOO PARLOR

*Write for information as to
availability*

DRAMATISTS PLAY SERVICE, Inc.
440 Park Avenue South   New York, N. Y. 10016

New
PLAYS

THE AMERICAN CLOCK
CHILDE BYRON
CLOSE OF PLAY
THE TRADING POST
THE LEGENDARY STARDUST BOYS
CLOSE TIES
OPAL'S MILLION DOLLAR DUCK
IN FIREWORKS LIE SECRET CODES
STOPS ALONG THE WAY
VILLAINOUS COMPANY
THE ACTOR'S NIGHTMARE

Inquiries Invited

DRAMATISTS PLAY SERVICE, INC.

440 Park Avenue South   New York, N. Y. 10016

New PLAYS

CHILDREN OF A LESSER GOD

PASSIONE

G. R. POINT

TIME AND GINGER

FATHERS AND SONS

THREE SISTERS

FULL MOON

THE ORPHANS

DUCK HUNTING

THE UBU PLAYS

TENNESSEE

THE COAL DIAMOND

WOMEN STILL WEEP

THE EXHIBITION

 DRAMATISTS PLAY SERVICE, INC.

440 Park Avenue South   New York, N. Y. 10016

New

TITLES

BURIED CHILD

TALLEY'S FOLLY

ARTICHOKE

THE TENNIS GAME

SAY GOODNIGHT, GRACIE

OLD PHANTOMS

FAMILY BUSINESS

LATER

MASTERPIECES

THE NATURE AND PURPOSE
    OF THE UNIVERSE;
  DEATH COMES TO US ALL,
    MARY AGNES;
  'DENTITY CRISIS (One Acts)

• *Write for Information*

DRAMATISTS PLAY SERVICE, INC.

440 Park Avenue South   New York, N.Y. 10016